MYCAMINO
WALK#2

18 pilgrims share their insights, their stories and their Camino journey

WRITING MATTERS PUBLISHING

My Camino Walk #2

First published in August 2018

Writing Matters Publishing (UK)
info@writingmatterspublishing.com
www.writingmatterspublishing.com

ISBN 978-1-912774-14-2 (Kindle)
ISBN 978-1-912774-15-9 (Pbk/Amazon)

Editor: Andrew Priestley

Contributors: Dan Mullins, Elaine Hopkins, Capitan Bradley, Emma Dunwoody, Deborah Kevin, Richard Brinton, Susie Gareh Minto, Julie Rogers, Callum Chambers, Angela Cummings, Heather Gauthier, Simon Jeffries, Marja Van Veen, Dave Sherlock-Jones, Alice Copilet, Adam Wells, John V Denley, Brad Genereux, Nancy Frey PhD, and Andrew Priestley.

This is dedicated to all pilgrims
on the *Camino de Santiago*
and on the *inner journey*
called the *Life Camino*.
Buen Camino!

Contents

Buen Camino!

Dan Mullins
(Radio producer, musician and presenter,
My Camino podcast)

One of the great things about the Camino is the lightbulb moment: "I'm walking."

You're a pilgrim.

Your family and friends may look at you a little askance when you tell them you're about to head to Europe to walk one of the many ancient, spiritual and mystical trails of the Camino de Santiago. Their confusion is somehow part of the allure. You tell them "I'm a pilgrim", with little understanding of how your life will change. Change is coming.

On the Way you'll find yourself alone with your thoughts, your failings, your doubts, your struggles. Then as a new day dawns you are refreshed, renewed, recharged.

The Camino gives us space and time. Space to love and leave; time to walk IN time with the rhythm of our hearts. If you truly believe in pilgrimage it is there, you'll find it.

As exhaustion kicks in, you realise you're alive with triumphs, achievements, singing, loving, learning and growing. Your heart will sing with the vigour of the journey. You will be challenged sure, but isn't that why we're here?

I sing a song about the Camino in pubs and clubs across Australia (details to follow, never miss a plug) and a woman approached me this week and said she would never be brave enough to walk the Camino.

The night ended with her hugging me yelling, 'I'm going!!!'.
I said, 'Buen Camino'.
She went off into the night to find out what I meant.

To all of you thinking of walking, be brave; to all of you who have walked, celebrate your bravery and long may you keep seeking and searching. You'll only discover if you're brave enough to search. And that is all part of the journey.

I hope you find what you're looking for somewhere along the Way.

The friends you make on the Camino will be friends for life - and what a wonderful life it is....

A pilgrim.

Walk on.

Go make history

Dan Mullins Sydney 2018

Link to Dan's podcast
https://www.whooshkaa.com/shows/my-camino-the-podcast
Link to the song *Somewhere Along the Way (the Camino Song)*
https://DanMullins.lnk.to/SomewhereAlongTheWay

Instagram - thesingingpilgrim
Facebook - @danmullinsmusic
Twitter - @2gbdanmullins
Webgsite - www.danmullinsmusic.com

The Camino At A Glance

Andrew Priestley

We are told that when James *(San Tiago)* was martyred in the Holy Land by Herod in 44AD his remains were transported by boat to Northern Spain. He was buried in a tomb but over time the tomb was lost and forgotten.

The story goes, around 813AD, a local shepherd was guided to a remote part of a dense wood where he discovered the lost tomb of San Tiago. The shepherd promptly informed the local bishop who in turn informed King Alfonso II The Chaste who made what is now called the first pilgrimage - the *Camino Primitivo*.

At first the tomb was a religious shrine and then a small cathedral was built to house the remains of St James the apostle of Christ. And quickly it became one of the great Catholic Holy pilgrimages for several hundred years.

From the 16th century onwards, however, due to church reform and wars, the Camino was inaccessible, or too dangerous and it fell out of favour. By the 20th century very few even remembered the route.

In the 1980s, a Catholic priest, Don Elias Valina Sampedro, researched the original route of the Camino and introduced yellow arrows to mark the various routes.

In 1987, around 2900 people registered to walk the Camino. The Camino has grown in popularity, and in 2017 over 300,000 people walked from ten official departure points for religious and non-religious reasons.

The peak period for the Camino appears to be between late March and October, with the most popular months being July, August and September (which probably coincides with late summer holidays in the northern hemisphere). The most comfortable months to walk the Camino appear to be Spring (March -May) and Autumn (September-October).

Statistics (2017) show that 27% of pilgrims are younger than 30 years of age, 55% are between 30-60, and 17% are 60+.

The key routes are *The French Camino - Camino Francés; The Camino Portugues, The Camino del Norte, Camino Primitivo, Camino Ingles* and *Via de la Plata*.

Over 25% of pilgrims start from Sarria, 100kms from Santiago, and 12% start from St Jean Pied de Port, the longest route, in France.

The Camino is an UNESCO-listed pilgrimage and is now considered one of the world's great walks.

My Camino Walk #2 follows hot on the heels of *My Camino Walk 1*. Both have become #1 bestselling *Travel and Tourism* books.

My Camino Walk 2 features the stories, insights and practical tips of 18 pilgrims. Once again, you are treated to an amazing cross-section of experiences that include the wondrous, the serendipitous, the miraculous and the challenging.

Pilgrims of all ages who walked alone, as couples and in groups. Pilgrims who walked for emotional hurts, physical pains, to raise money for charity and to raise spirits.

Game-changing to life-changing.

Once again we invite you to share their stories, their adventures, their insights, their practical advice and wisdom. But ultimately their inspiration. If you are thinking of walking the Camino, this is the perfect place to start.

Buen Camino!

Living Beyond Labels

Elaine Hopkins

The first time I'm on the Camino it's by accident.

Aged 57, I've decided to study Spanish to stave off Alzheimer's. Desperate for an opportunity to practise the lingo with the locals before I sit my exams, I sign up for a Spanish cycling tour that coincides with my college holidays. I barely notice that the tour follows the course of this path called the Camino de Santiago: from Léon to Santiago de Compostela.

As I ride and push my bike up some humongous ascents and freewheel the descents, I have some amazing experiences.

Fittingly, since I'm on the Camino by accident, I also have an accident. My bum and my bicycle part company. I end up head-first, face-down on the side of a steep drainage ditch. I stop breathing. I almost die.

Had it not been for the intervention of Bob, an ex-SAS Lieutenant-Colonel and cycling tour companion, I would have died.

I'm no stranger to accidents.

I suffer from dyspraxia, a life-long neurological condition that can affect movement, co-ordination, balance, memory, motor skills, and speech. In my case, I have a dysfunctional relationship with gravity, balance, and direction.

This accident changes me - and not just physically.

My face will never be the same again - the left side is dented and marked - and neither will my knees, now enhanced by an attractive criss-cross pattern. But this is as nothing compared with the mental and emotional effects of the accident.

For the first time in four decades, I'm no longer afraid of death.

Had I died that day, I would have left this earth happy, doing something I loved doing. Were I to be given the opportunity to craft my own death, I couldn't have designed a better way to go.

Letting go of this fear makes a huge difference to my everyday experience, but there's more to come. I discover that fears are like slices of bread in a pop-up toaster: no sooner does one appear than a second follows.

It's no surprise to me that my second biggest fear is that of public speaking, an activity I've avoided all my life. But that was my pre-Camino life; once the Camino brings something to your attention, it's almost impossible to ignore it. So I don't.

I enroll on an inspiring speaking course.

On day one, I've done my pre-course homework. I've prepared a two-minute speech; my subject is my Camino cycling accident. The course leader is a man called Adam and there are 12 students. Imagine my surprise when Adam introduces himself as someone who runs a Camino business. Two out of 12 people talking about the Camino de Santiago? It's hardly a mainstream interest in the UK, but, on this particular day, it is.

By the time the course ends six months later, I know a lot more about the Camino because I know Adam better. I also know a lot more about myself, having unearthed a natural talent for public speaking, a talent that has lain dormant and buried under all that fear for all those years.

At the same time as I'm studying public speaking I'm also studying neuroscience. One day, my neuroscience professor says to me: 'Whenever there's a deficit in one part of the brain, there'll be a compensating abundance in another.'

The thought piques my interest in passing, only to disappear in the mental flotsam and jetsam of the day.

It returns a couple of days later when I'm doing nothing in particular, and this time it sticks. I realise that my compensating abundance for my dyspraxia is my gift with words.

A fully formed question snags my brain: *Would you be prepared to sacrifice your ability with words if you knew it would banish the dyspraxia?*

The answer is both immediate and forceful: *No.*

In that moment, I feel things shift within me: I begin to accept my dyspraxia instead of resenting it.

Later that day, still doing nothing, I stare at the fire and the television. I zoom forward 20 years. I'm still staring at the fire and the television.

Sh*t, if I don't do something different, this is it. This is all there is.

I'm so angry with myself that I fling my slippers and the remote control at the television. I'm angry at the realisation that I've allowed my physically active life to narrow. To nothing.

I've allowed the back pain and the chronic migraines that have dogged my life for the past 30 years to gain the upper hand. And I've spent those years expecting someone else to fix my health issues, rather than assuming responsibility for them myself. Even my love affair with cycling is a cover-up for the fact that I can no longer walk more than half a mile without suffering excruciating pain.

Remembering the Biblical injunction not to let the sun go down on my anger, I go to bed in a calmer frame of mind - and with a vague sense that I'll know what to do in the morning.

What? screams my logical mind. *You want to return to the Camino? You've been there once before and you nearly died. Now you want to take up long-distance backpacking as a cure for your chronic ill-health?*

My logical mind has a point; it's a good one, but I ignore it. The message from my instinct is so strong that I don't fret about my lack of experience or fitness. I go straight into making it happen mode.

I ask Adam if he'll teach me everything I need to know and accompany me for the first week.

I find an osteopath and a personal trainer, and I sign up for a five-mile guided walk the next weekend. I doubt whether I can walk five miles; I haven't walked that far in decades. But I do it with ease, and my joy overflows. I still don't know what was at work that day.

Maybe accepting responsibility for my own health is the act of self-love that changed everything; maybe my instinct-inspired motivation to revisit the Camino is so strong that it overcomes every obstacle.

Whatever happened, I continue training, reconnecting with my childhood love of walking.

And so it is that, on 7 May 2014, three years after my cycling accident and five months after my slipper-chucking moment, Adam and I set off from St Jean Pied de Port heading for Logroño. As we undertake our first day, 26 km across the Pyrenees to Roncesvalles, I feel as though I've been released into the wild. I'm back in my natural habitat, after being caged in corporate life for 35 years. Adam helps me when the terrain becomes tricky, but I still manage to have an accident.

On day two while sightseeing, I fall over on the *Bridge of Rabies* in Zubiri; that's the one with the alleged curative properties. I attempt to hide this accident from Adam. As I pick myself up, I realise I'm ashamed of my dyspraxia. It makes no sense: dyspraxia is just part of my genetic inheritance, but shame is a very distinctive, very heavy, very visceral emotion - and I feel it.

We cover the 160 km between St Jean and Logroño in seven days, including one 40 km day. Apart from a few blisters, I suffer no health issues: no back pain, no migraines. I'm going to have to stop labelling myself as a chronically ill individual who can't walk.

I return home, thinking I'm done with the Camino, but the Camino isn't done with me. About ten days later, in the midst of some freelance copywriting, my fingers wander off and book a return flight to Spain and renew my travel insurance.

My other-than-conscious mind has decided that I'm going back to the Camino. And this time I'm going back to make peace with my dyspraxia.

I resume in Logroño expecting to walk the remaining 630 km by myself, but, on my second day, I meet an American pilgrim called Anna and we start walking together.

The first thing I learn about her is that she's a coach, as am I; the second is that she's dyspraxic, as am I. I have what I can only describe as a McEnroe moment.

I cast my eyes heavenwards:

You cannot be serious. I've come back to the Camino with the express purpose of making peace with my dyspraxia, and you give me another dyspraxic as a walking companion. How the hell is that going to work?

It works perfectly.

I've never spent time with another dyspraxic before, and it turns out to be one of the most healing experiences of my life.

Anna does all the things I do: trips, stumbles, bangs into furniture, slips on floors, drops objects. We laugh at and with one another.

Anna and I walk together for three weeks, and it's almost as though the Camino is challenging me to revisit, review and let go of the labels that have defined my life.

In Villafranca Montes de Oca, Anna accepts an invitation to another pilgrim's birthday party on our behalf. As a career introvert, I work myself into a frenzy, but I realise I have a choice. I can either choose to be curious about the other guests, or I can lapse into my belief that I'm such an introvert that I'm socially inept. I choose the former and, guess what? I have an enjoyable evening.

On the steep and treacherous descent into Molinaseca which is a challenge for most pilgrims and an accident-waiting-to-happen for two dyspraxics on the Camino, I take command. I tell Anna we're not starting until we've rested, taken on food and water, and achieved an appropriate mental state. And there's to be no talking on the way down either. Well, that dispels the label that says I can never be a leader.

After 34 days on the Camino Francés, I feel not so much refreshed and renewed as remade. I've lived beyond so many of my self-imposed labels: chronically ill, unable to walk long distances, socially awkward, incapable of leadership. But what about the biggest label of all, the one that's dominated my life? What about the dyspraxia?

That's the greatest gift of all - and I don't even know I've received it until I start practising my returned pilgrim speech for the annual *Pilgrim Day* at the Confraternity of Saint James in London.

I decide to make a joke about not knowing my right hand from my left. And it won't matter which hand I use to signal right and left because I've never known the difference - at least not without considering the matter very, very deeply for a good five minutes. I start to make the joke. And then stop. I sink to the floor and end up in the prayer position. I look in amazement at what I now know - with absolute certainty - is my right hand.

My hand hasn't changed, but what has changed are the neural pathways in my brain. Focusing on walking and interpreting waymarks during my Camino has activated my neural plasticity: the brain's ability to reorganise itself by forming new neural connections in response to new situations or changes in the environment. I've laid down new neural paths that enable me to distinguish instinctively and immediately between my right hand and my left.

I've never, ever believed that this could be possible. For me, it's a minor miracle. And it's a minor miracle that's given new meaning to my life. I continue to walk pilgrim paths every year to see how else I can rewire my brain, and I also speak, write, and coach others about how we can all live beyond our labels.

About Elaine Hopkins

Elaine Hopkins is an award-winning speaker and writer who walked the Camino Francés over five weeks in the summer of 2014.

Before walking the Camino, she was a coach and a copywriter. Elaine's experience on the Camino changed her so profoundly that she now spends her time more creatively: walking pilgrim paths, and speaking, writing, and coaching about our ability to live beyond our labels and step into our potential.

Since her first Camino, Elaine has walked the *Camino Inglés* (Ferrol to Santiago), the *Via Podiensis* (Le Puy to St Jean), from her home in London to Santiago, the *Camino Portugués* (Porto to Santiago), the *Camino Sanabrés* (Ourense to Santiago), as well as parts of the *Vía de la Plata*, the *Camino Ignaciano,* and the *Vézelay* route.

In all, she has walked more than 5,000 pain-free kilometres on European pilgrim paths which isn't bad for someone who couldn't walk a single kilometre without pain when she first decided to take to the Camino in 2014.

The first volume of Elaine's Camino memoir is due to be published by *writingmatterspublishing.com* in 2019.

You can find out more about Elaine here:

http://elainehopkinsauthor.com

Follow her Camino adventures here:

Facebook: https://www.facebook.com/
dailydiscoverieswithelaine/

Instagram: https://www.instagram.com/
elainehopkins_writerandwalker/

My Camino 2015-2017

Capitan Bradley

The Camino de Santiago, specifically the French route, is a very special and deeply personal place to me. It gave me the ideal travel experiences and opportunities to reflect alone and with others about life there and life back at home.

The pilgrimage gives you a perspective about yourself and others that no other travel nor mundane routine back home could possibly deliver.

Spain and those drawn to her are simply unique.

My Camino literally came calling in early 2015 via our oldest daughter. She was graduating with her Masters in Education in a few months and I received a call from her selling me on this special experience.

I grew up in the church, and grew old in it too, before walking away from organized religion in my mid-40's.

Over all of those decades in the church, I had never heard of the Camino de Santiago nor any of the major Christian pilgrimages. I knew about those of the Jewish faith going to Jerusalem and those of Islamic faith going to Mecca.

However, my Christian teachings never shared such a thing with me. It took my grown daughter to enlighten me and, after a little research and watching Emilio Estavez and Martin Sheen in *The Way* movie, I jumped on the opportunity.

Fairly quickly, we were booked on a plane and were gearing

up and I began walking daily for months to prepare for our July, 2015 departure from the US to Paris to Madrid and then on to Leon via train. Leon was only two weeks of walking away from Santiago de Compostela, which fit our schedules the best. 300kms over two weeks also seemed like an ideal distance and time to challenge a dad in his late 40's and his early 20's daughter. We had never spent such nonstop time together, since she was a child.

We arrived and found our way around Spain quite easily, especially so since my daughter is fluent in Spanish.

With my trusted Brierly guidebook, I was our guide through smaller towns and villages, where the pilgrim crowds are much smaller and the communal dinners and conversations really led to great afternoons and evenings along our Camino.

I had traveled around North America, the Caribbean, and Hawaii, but never to Europe.

This was quite the introduction to such a great country and new continent. We walked anywhere from 15km to 33km per day, averaging 23km per day, taking breaks along the way to eat, rest, and find a bathroom, as needed. We stayed in 15 different albergues, hotels, and B&Bs during our time in Spain ... another first for any trip we've ever taken. Different places, different spaces, rooms full of bunk beds, private rooms to ourselves, meals for two and communal meals with many.

Each day and night was an adventure and one to figure out each day without reservations and any certainty that we had made the best choice.

We just let the Camino and our guidebook lead our instincts and hunches to where we thought we could start at sunrise and be finished walking by lunchtime. Showers, lunch, and naps were to follow each day, along with physical recovery, more food, and vino tinto and/or cervesas. Lots of cheap and delicious vino tinto and cervesas flowed those afternoons and evenings, which aided in our daily recovery and conversations with each other and new friends, hosts, and fellow pilgrims. This was no vacation. It was even better.

This Camino was as perfect as it could be.

The people we met along *The Way* were of like spirit and were just as adventurous. The food we ate was delicious and simple, as were the drinks we enjoyed.

The weather over those two weeks was perfect. Not a drop of rain with cool, crisp mornings followed by hot afternoons, after we had arrived at our next town. Leon to Santiago started out flat and pastoral as far as we could see and then transformed in Galicia into more rugged and mountainous terrain that was as gorgeous as it was challenging. We listened to our bodies, mainly knees and feet, and we relaxed daily, as needed.

Walking for just 5-6 hours and then resting for 18-19 hours every day was our constant goal and routine. Sunrise to noon was our goal each day, but you can't always control the distance between targeted towns and villages. We just did our best to walk, talk, not talk, and stay connected as father and daughter and people of a simpler side of earth.

Loss also seems to be a frequent challenge for many of us who were taking on the Camino with us.

Ginny and I had both lost our fathers in 2013 and those losses still hurt, and still do today. It's no fun being the patriarch of our side of the family in your mid-40's, especially when you've lost so much in less than a decade. Fathers, business partners, mentor, attorney and friend, and other friends dropping in their prime of life. Mid-life is the beginning of serious losses and, I believe, the beginning of our own end. My Camino gave me another beginning and I'm grateful for that.

Others we met were struggling with losses of love, jobs, careers, material wealth, and on and on. Loss of oneself, as well. That felt like me.

Of course, this first Camino was not just about me. It was about her, our daughter, and what was probably the last time we would ever spend like this again. She had found her new love and they were married the following year. This was our last time together like this. Both of our girls were now grown women with great guys and I grieved that loss as a father along with our excitement of their solid loves and relationships. But, those little girls were gone now and add more losses to my book of life.

We returned and the post-Camino feeling most report did not really take hold with me. I was glad to be home with those I love and missed. However, I have thought about the Camino everyday since and probably will for the rest of my life. Thanks to *YouTube*, I can live any day vicariously on the Camino with any number of singles and groups from all around the globe. That's part of the Camino magic.

After moving our family to a beautiful part of the American heartland, our daughter's wedding, and the election of the worst human being ever to occupy the White House, I had a physical breakdown of sorts that led me back to the Camino.

Ginny encouraged me to do what I needed to do to return to better physical, mental, and emotional health. Only she and I knew what I was dealing with in March of 2017. I did just what I needed to do, with her love and support. I stopped one bad habit and my recovery began.

My next Camino was next and I walked every fair to brilliant day to gear up my body for what I knew was to come.

Our second summer in our new hometown passed and I was returning to Spain by myself, with no translator daughter to help along *The Way*. I would be fine. Delta got me there and a challenging bus find finally dropped me off in Burgos this time for the month of August, 2017.

All alone, I walked out of the bus station with just my backpack and headed to the old town center. There, I found the lovely old city and trappings of such a nice, historic, and giving city of Burgos.

I began my first day as more of a tourist than a pilgrim. I found my Marriott AC hotel right there on the canal and it was a perfect, quiet, and classy start to my pilgrimage.

Full breakfast the next morning proved that again, as my solo pilgrimage began. This time is was 500km to Santiago, over about three weeks of walking plus rest days.

Burgos is the beginning of the second of three legs of the Camino Frances. The start in France and across the Pyrenees mountains to Burgos is the first leg or what I've heard termed the birth or life phase. Burgos to Leon is on the Meseta, mainly farmland and higher plateaus and the death phase. Leon to Galicia and on to Santiago is varied terrain and beautiful and the rebirth or resurrection phase, for those who believe in the Christian metaphor.

Someday, I will be able to invest the entire five weeks needed to take on the entire *Camino Frances* with my loved ones. That is one of my dreams, along with the *Camino Portuguese, Camino Norte*, and *Camino Primotivo*.

Burgos to Hontanas, my first day, was about 32km in the sunny Meseta and I was practically hallucinating as I entered town. Cold aqua never tasted so good, as did the tall cervesa in my hilltop albergue's courtyards. Many courtyards, cold cervesas and vino tintos were in my future this Camino.

Each day was full of great walks, talks, new friends, reunions of sorts, and great food and conversations at all points along my *Way*.

All I had to concern myself with was my health, comfort, well-being, and making quick friends with others who were looking for the same.

My 2017 Camino was not full of loss, as much as it was full of life, love, and like-minded singles and couples. So many happy couples! Refreshing, but really had me missing Ginny and her experiencing my new friends from Brazil, from Turin in North Italy, and another great couple from Boston. Happy, fellow Americans on the Camino are pretty rare. That's fine. I like happy pilgrims from all around the world, which are all over the Camino.

Most of all, outside of the fun, food, and libations shared along my Way, I found a deep desire to talk to God again. Not the usual blessing at the dinner table and our kids' bedsides, but walking into small churches and huge cathedrals, alike, to look, admire, be mindful, and pray for forgiveness, for thankfulness, and for blessings upon all who I love and adore. God was speaking to me like never before. I felt it in my mind, heart, and my somehow pain-free knees. God was continuing to work with me and I was grateful. Life led me to that *Man of a Certain Age* place. God led me back to the Camino. One happy pilgrim here and I had never prayed so much everyday in my entire life.

Suffice it to say, I finished that 500km Camino with new friends to visit someday and several host friends to look forward to seeing again with each *Camino Frances* I take on in the future. Other Camino routes to take on and I hope to walk each one with those I love and maybe with those who we have met and keep meeting. Maybe Camino reunions are in our future, since typical family reunions are rare and don't seem to be as fulfilling. Maybe we all should consider our Camino family as our renewal reunion every year or two. I like that plan.

If your Camino is calling you, just go. Make the time happen. Make time for yourself and/or with loved ones. Do the 5-day from Sarria, the 13-day from Leon, the 21-day from Burgos, or the 30-day across the entire *Camino Frances* … just do it, with rest days allotted. Whether you are spiritual or not, your long walks will build your strength in many ways and should leave you a very different person.

Buen Camino.

About Capitan Bradley

Capitan is another middle-aged husband, father of four, happy cook, future cruising sailor, an amateur writer and self-publisher of the *Man of A Certain Age* book series, and a hopeless lover of Spain and her people, villages, cuisine, and vino tinto.

After 20 years of entrepreneurial experiences, Bradley walked away to focus on managing the family homestead for his successful partner and wonderful wife, Ginny, and their two teenage boys.

His walks along the Camino de Santiago in 2015, with his oldest daughter, and then starting solo in 2017 were two of the most meaningful and transformational times of his life. Both Caminos offered very different experiences and times for renewal and recovery.

With plans to return in 2019 and hopefully every other year thereafter, his need to return tells the tale of this historic and beautiful trail's impact on his heart, soul, body, and mind.

This Man of a Certain Age is now in a much better place and wants to share his story with other challenged souls.

Facebook: Capitan Brad @ https://www.facebook.com/
LeadFollowOrGetOutOfTheWay
Twitter: @JustBeCauseTwit
Blog: https://justbecausetwit.wordpress.com

Finding ME

Emma Dunwoody

I decided 2018 was to be the year of me. The time to rediscover who I am and what makes my heart sing.

I am a 43 year old mother of two, entrepreneur, coach, mentor, wife and strung-out human being and although I had a life full of people and experiences I enjoyed and even love, I felt my life was not fulfilling.

I realised that I was living the life I felt I should be living and not a life that felt inspirational and connected to my heart.

I had long known of the Camino and was curious to do it. However, I had held myself back from committing because of fear.

My excuses were many: "I couldn't leave the kids. My husband couldn't take care of the kids and his work with me away for that long. I couldn't afford it".

So I shelved it and told myself maybe when the kids are older or we have more money.

Until one day in early January this year sitting in our bedroom in tears, I had shared with my husband that I had been feeling the ticking of time, that I thought life would be different by now and that I felt terribly guilty saying it but I was feeling unfulfilled and afraid that perhaps I had missed my opportunity to be who I once dreamed of being.

I was feeling stuck and uninspired in my life and this had

to be the year of rediscovering me, finding inspiration and fulfilment.

In that moment my husband asked, "What would make you feel fulfilled?" I didn't know the answer to that but what came out was, "I feel drawn to walk the Camino this year."

I expected all the excuses and reasons why I couldn't do it to come out of his mouth but they didn't.

"OK, book your ticket, right now, and we'll work it out".

In that moment, I knew the excuses were just that and they had just been dealt with head on, I had said yes to the Camino and I was all in.

The week before leaving for the Camino was intense. My ego had incredible stories of everything that could go wrong and I couldn't shake the fate of the son in the movie *The Way* with Martin Sheen and Emilio Estevez. I feared for my safety at times. I'm a mother of two boys: *what was I doing?*

I share this with you because I realised on reflection that we are so paralysed by the labels we wear, by our identity, that it can be confronting and very difficult to follow our heart when our ego tells us how crazy we are and all the possible things that could go wrong.

It takes bravery and courage to take that first step, to make the decision and follow through, especially being a mother, wife and business owner with responsibilities to other human lives, but make no mistake this was the best decision of my life, to face the fear, to sit in the discomfort and to say yes to the Camino.

As I began the Camino I noticed my usual confidence was lacking its usual clarity and I was choosing to rely on others and ask for help, something that doesn't always occur to a high achieving, busy mother of two, who's pretty much always in control.

I'm used to solving problems on my own and just getting on with it. However, almost instantly I realised I was

not the expert, I was not able to solve this all on my own and I certainly was not in control.

The first 24 hours, leaving from St Jean Pied de Port, crossing over the Pyrenees and into Roncesvalles was incredibly challenging. We encountered extreme weather with cold winds and rain and as we climbed we experienced fog that kept our vision no more than four meters ahead of us, continued temperature drops, high winds and more rain.

Then as we crossed along the top it began to snow.

When we were reaching the top of the climb I was so cold my hands were blue, my whole body was tired and the conditions had really affected my attitude. It's fair to say I was not having much fun.

We saw a sign that told us we still had another 10kms to go and my heart dropped.

Just keep going, I kept telling myself, *there is no turning back now.*

We rounded a corner and my mood shifted, there was a truck with a shelter, snacks and hot chocolate, I couldn't believe it, what was this guy doing out here in the middle of nowhere in this weather with food and hot chocolate?

"Thank goodness, my saviour", I thought.

It was the best hot chocolate I have ever had and I thanked the guy so fervently that I nearly shook his arm right out of its socket, I wanted him to know he had changed everything for me and I now had the energy to see the bright side: we were in France, walking the Camino, how good it was to feel excited again.

You see, often you will be pushed to your limits on the Camino, as I was on the first day and, just when you think that it's beaten you something magical happens to change your experience.

On the Camino there is a saying *The Camino provides, we are being taken care of on this pilgrimage and you will always be given what you need, even if it's a lesson or fear that it's time to overcome and grow into a new version of you.*

I was asked once when interviewed about my Camino experience: did you get out unscathed? I answered honestly "Oh no, definitely not, but I loved every minute of it".

After the challenge of day one I knew I was capable of this adventure.

The first ten days were filled with beautiful landscapes, meeting incredible people and a lot of body pain as I became *Camino fit,* which in the beginning you think will never happen but one day you just stop thinking about your body and your focus becomes more about your thoughts and your life at home.

I met some amazing people along *The Way.* We shared so many stories, tears and laughter and became close as if we had

MY CAMINO WALK #2

known each other for years not days. As a friend of mine says, *They become your Camino family, and just like a real family you are there for each other, you learn to trust each other, share your fears, struggles, dreams and hopes* and for me I felt honoured to be a part of this incredible life changing Camino journey with these beautiful humans.

These people inspired me, made me laugh and cry. I was endlessly curious about them and their reasons for being on the Camino.

Each night I loved to come together and ask them what they had learned today, what had they heard and shared? I found in everyone's stories there was a lesson or resonance for me, making me feel as if I am connected to these people, this pilgrimage and of course the rest of the world. We all fear the same things, we all dream the same dreams, we all want to be seen and loved.

Incredibly, on the Camino, vulnerability is cool. No one is talking about business or making money. No, we are all there for much bigger reasons.

I was there to discover myself again after 18 years of marriage, kids and working to create something for our family, and for others. It was healing from broken relationships, leaving behind old jobs to discover something new and to rediscover adventure and human connection.

The beauty of all this is I became connected to ME again, to my heart, my soul, my purpose and I rediscovered her in a big way through these people. We see ourselves in them reflected back at us, the Emma these people see is vibrant, curious, fun loving, a free spirit, wise and deeply connected, she is just the Emma I had been missing for so long, the freedom of being me, like Alice in Wonderland on her way down the rabbit hole.

These people, my Camino family, helped me rediscover myself and be more ME.

We arrived in Leon on Day 21 and by this stage our group was spread over a number of days, so I and another friend stayed

for a rest day to recharge our tired bodies and to catch up with friends both nights. On the second night we sat in the plaza in front of the Cathedral discussing how we'd been and what we'd learned with our friends Ollie and Justine.

Ollie turns to me and says, "I've noticed a pattern amongst the walkers, there are three groups that walk everyday. Group 1 want to be first. They leave early, walk fast and love to win. Group 2 get up early. They walk as a group and they keep going until they reach their destination and secure their bed because they believe that is what they have to do as a pilgrim. And Group 3, get up late, often walk alone, go at their own pace and have this faith that they will get a bed at the end of the day."

"No group is better or worse, it's just the one you feel most comfortable in."

This blew my mind. He was right and I realised that the frustration I had been experiencing, especially crossing the Meseta, was because I had been first in Group 1 and then 2, but I realised I in fact belonged in Group 3. The final insight he offered was, *we walk as we work* and yes, again Ollie was right.

The following day I consciously chose to be a Group 3 walker to see if my intuition was correct and that I would be a lot happier alone, walking at my own pace and with faith that my bed will be there.

That's when everything changed.

This shift of slowing down, walking alone and listening to my own internal guidance system changed my Camino experience significantly, it was as if I came home and was in a continual flow state, just beautiful.

From that point it was as if the colour was turned up, the animals were characters in a story and each conversation was a delight to be savoured - the Camino came alive.

I appreciate I have not shared with you much of the actual walking, countryside or daily experience, but for me the Camino is about spirit, about the soul and reconnecting to her. Besides there will be plenty more people in this book sharing the villages and the food.

I want you to know about how the Camino changes you. She looks into your soul and helps to chip away the armour you have built up over the years, the armour preventing you from hearing who you really are and what makes your heart sing.

As we walk each day we have the opportunity to live a whole life, to discover how you have been doing life at home and better still how you want to be living your life. The Camino is a metaphor for life, how you walk is how you live and if you don't like the way you're walking then change it until your heart sings, as mine did the day I learnt I was a Group 3 walker.

Now home I walk to my own rhythm, I choose to be alone as much as being with others and I have changed my life to fit my way of walking instead of my life dictating the way I walk through it.

Whatever this book inspires in you go do it ... *right now!!*
Buen Camino

About Emma Dunwoody

Emma is a surfer, pilgrim, mother, wife, coach and writer so inspired by the Camino and her life-changing experience she now takes groups back a number of times a year to coach them through the process she designed on her pilgrimage.

She discovered her purpose, mission and who she is in her soul while waking the Camino and believes she is here to share the same opportunity for others to know themselves this way.

Her blog *alifethruinsta.com* shares with readers all her journeys while trying to makes sense of this adventure called life.

Website; https://alifethruinsta.com/
Insta; https://www.instagram.com/emma_dunwoody/
Facebook; https://www.facebook.com/emma.dunwoody.5
LinkedIn; https://www.linkedin.com/in/
emma-dunwoody-b8311356/

Call Of The Camino

Deborah Kevin

I met Heather Waring in November 2016 when she sat down next to me after a break at a business owner's meeting held in Ft. Lauderdale, Florida. The room teemed with people, some of whom I knew, most of whom I didn't.

"What's your business?" I asked after our preliminary introductions. I learned she lived in London but was Northern Irish. She learned I was a Philadelphian transplanted to Baltimore.

"I lead women on the Camino," she said.

"You're kidding me."

For years I'd been telling my family that I wanted to walk the Camino de Santiago. I peppered her with questions.

Heather jotted down her website address, clearly delighted with my interest. "Not many Americans know about the Camino."

I confessed that before seeing the movie *The Way*, I hadn't heard of it either. I could hardly wait to research her. The Universe had connected us for a reason, and I knew I would join her.

After lunch, I scoured the room for Heather. I spotted that bright scarf and made a beeline for her. She looked up as my words rushed out. "I'm coming with you."

She looked gobsmacked. "Really? That's wonderful!"

I had difficulty focusing. All I could think about was the Camino. I wanted to prove to myself that I could do it, despite being over 50 and overweight. My ex-husband had laughed at my declaration that I'd hike the Camino someday. His decade-long cruelty was in my rearview mirror, but I hadn't completely healed.

For six months, I walked daily and hiked on weekends. The local hiking specialty shop measured me for a backpack and new hiking shoes. I purchased trekking poles, socks, and waterproofs. I built up my endurance and wore my new shoes all day, every day. I joined a club and hiked all kinds of terrain for varying distances, gradually bulking up my backpack.

I'd been hiking all my life, so I was confident in my ability. My family stills whispers of how when I was four years old, I walked ten miles in the Wisconsin Dells. More recently, I hiked in the Swiss Alps, the Rockies, and the San Juan Mountains.

By the time I boarded my flight to Paris, I felt prepared. I successfully navigated Charles de Gaulle airport and five trains to arrive in Cahors, France—and all with a limited French vocabulary. The entire trip took more than twenty-four hours.

Outside the Cahors train depot, I discovered embedded in the sidewalk a Camino shell. Travel-weariness faded as my excitement grew. The shell markers led me into the town, across a bridge, and to my hotel.

I ought to have taken a nap, but I couldn't sleep. Instead, I walked about Cahors, exploring its alleys in search of the Cathédrale Saint-Étienne. I wanted to obtain my Camino passport, though Heather warned me that it was unlikely I'd get one until Saint-Jean-Pied-de-Port.

As I poked around the ancient building, I came across a flyer announcing when the Camino passports would be available. A quick glance at my watch indicated only a short wait, and one I was willing to make.

My passport secured, I met up with the other five women, who'd arrived from London.

That evening, we enjoyed a celebratory dinner over which we declared our individual intentions for the five-day trek.

Darkness fell. We trundled to bed, hoping for a good night's sleep.

The sun rose in a cloudless sky, and fog hovered just above the surface of the Lot River. It was a perfect morning to begin our trek, just chilly enough to require a light fleece. We scarfed down a light breakfast, chugged tepid coffee, and donned our packs. I noticed with alarm that my backpack was more than double the size of the other women's, and it was stuffed full, weighing forty pounds.

The Valentré Bridge, famous as one of the Devil's bridges, was the ceremonial start to our Camino journey. Heather regaled our group with its history before we crossed the river, pausing midway to snap photos. Our excitement was palpable.

Just across the bridge, a granite outcropping rose above us. A collective groan escaped our lips. The hillside had steep, narrow steps carved into it. My pack's weight combined with my short legs made the ascent difficult. Thorns snatched at me. At one point, I crawled upward on my hands and knees because the steepness combined with the drop-off had me panicking. I found myself wishing for mountain goat ancestry.

We reached the summit and traversed a short path to arrive at a clearing. An iron cross jutted fifteen feet in the sky. We dropped our packs at its base, chugged water, and caught our breath.

At the cliff's edge, a sweeping view of Cahors lay at my feet, and the Valentré Bridge looked tiny spanning the winding river. The image confirmed how far we'd come in a short while. Doubts crept into my mind. Had I bitten off more than I could handle? I castigated myself for having overpacked. Closing my eyes, I took in deep breaths. You've got to believe you can do this. Trust that the call you feel is real and for a reason.

Ten hours and twenty miles later, we still had four and a half miles farther to go until we'd reach Montcuq. I paused to gulp down tepid water and said a silent prayer for having made it that far. Onward!

I fell last in line to cross a balance beam of hard-packed earth. Waist-high fronds on my left shimmered in the light breeze.

A gully of mud was to my right. I teetered. My foot slipped into the sludge. My ankle twisted. Ping. A shockwave ran up my right leg. I paused, sucking air deep into my lungs. Not my knee! No! But I said nothing, pushing through the pain that grew with each footstep. I fell further behind the others as we plodded toward Montcuq.

"Debby, you're really limping," one of the women named Roz said. She'd waited for me to catch up to her. "Do you need help?"

I said, "We're almost to the hotel. I'm sure I can make it."

In truth, doubts about my ability to finish not only the day but the entire Camino ping-ponged inside my head. "I have a knee brace I can put on once we're there." My knees, riddled with arthritis from years of ski and bike injuries, were likely overdue for surgery. In truth, my pain mirrored my internal scarring, making visible the spiritual hurt I limped through life carrying.

Roz insisted that I stop. "You'll only cause more damage if you wait."

I knew she was right. Dropping my overstuffed pack on the road, I ruched around until I unearthed the neoprene brace and clamped it on. Using my walking sticks like crutches, I hobbled along, Roz by my side the entire way.

Daylight waned as we twisted down narrow streets. I gritted my teeth and prayed with each step that we were near our B&B, which was at the far end of town. Each turn only revealed long stretches of road lined with centuries-old houses. Lights flared to life inside windows as the sun disappeared.

We turned a corner to finally arrive at our hotel. It had been an exhausting day, more grueling than any of us had expected. We arrived an hour after dinner time, which on the Camino meant you didn't eat. To our intense gratitude and relief, the owners had waited for us.

By the time my roommate and I retired, it was nearly eleven. We still had to elevate our legs to drain lactic acid, a hiker's trick to avoid cramped muscles. When I pulled off my hiking boots and peeled away my thick socks, I discovered a blister the size of a quarter on my left heel. Never before had my feet blistered.

I searched in vain for Band-Aids in my backpack's main compartment. Nothing. In a side pocket, I found blister plasters. Heather had given them to me a day earlier, and I'd taken them to be polite. I didn't get blisters.

The next morning dawned sunny and chilly. After a pilgrim's breakfast of freshly baked bread and raspberry jam, we hit the trail. I felt determined despite the dull throb of my knee and rub of my blister. Periodic worries about permanent knee damage snaked their way into my otherwise cheerful thoughts. I pushed them aside and focused on the birdcalls and warmth of the sun.

After about five miles, we came upon a small stone chapel whose doors were flung open.

We ditched our packs on the picnic table outside and wandered into the dark church. A placard indicated it had been built in 982CE. Peeling frescos in shades of umber and mustard covered the walls. Golden stars sparkled on a midnight ceiling. An emaciated Christ hung on a freestanding cross next to the raised altar, photos, withered flowers and candles at its base. Dust adorned the silk flowers tucked into an alcove.

I sank into one of the hard wooden chairs, slipping into silent prayer. *Thank you for bringing me this far. Thank you for helping me to continue. Please ease my pain. Help me understand what my lesson is.*

I felt a hand on my shoulder and opened my eyes. Heather indicated I should follow her outside.

"Debby, I'm quite worried about your knee. Would you be okay with me ordering a taxi to take you to our hotel for the night?" Heather asked, her voice kind. "I don't want you to get worse. Perhaps having a bit of a lie-in will make you fit to continue tomorrow."

Tears formed at the corners of my eyes. I didn't want to give up, but I knew my desire put everyone else behind schedule. I also knew Heather was right. The pain was excruciating, I couldn't speak, so I nodded my agreement.

Heather folded me in her arms, whispering in my ear, "You of all people. You've been so looking forward to this trip, and you trained so hard." She hugged me tighter.

It turns out finding a taxi in rural France isn't easy, especially on a Saturday afternoon of a holiday weekend.

Thankfully, it wasn't impossible, and before long a van appeared. I hoisted myself into the front seat.

My friends waved until we disappeared.

Upon arrival at the farmhouse, I popped a painkiller and slid between crisp sheets under a plump duvet. Thoughts thumped through my brain to the rhythm of my heartbeat: *My ex-husband was right. I couldn't walk the Camino. I should have prepared better. What's with the blisters?* My eyes closed and I fell into a dreamless sleep.

I awoke in the late afternoon to the sound of children playing. A breeze blew through the open window caressing my face. I recalled my last thoughts and felt embarrassed at having given in to them. Stop *should-ing* on yourself. You did your best. No one could have predicted that you'd slip. Of course, you WILL complete the Camino. Tomorrow's a new day.

The next morning, I liberally rubbed on muscle cream and slid the brace over my knee. I felt ready to be back on the trail. Days three through five started the same way: rising by 6am to breakfast and hitting the trail by 8am. We passed through ancient towns that had been Roman fortresses, walked along a canal for an entire day, and slid down wet leaves along mud paths. The smell of freshly mown grass lingered in the air filled with the song of countless unseen birds.

Trekking part of the Camino was the most strenuous activity I've ever undertaken. My blisters grew to the size of silver dollars, and my knees twinged the entire way. But the peace, quiet, and time to reflect was a priceless gift.

I can hardly wait for the next leg!

About Deborah Kevin

Deborah Kevin (pronounced *key-vin*) father's military career had her family moving so often that she attended 13 schools in 12 years.

While it was difficult growing up as the perpetual new girl, she's grateful for the skills she learned: flexibility, adaptability, and the ability to listen.

Deborah works with visionary entrepreneurs who are out to make an impact on our world and their communities. She helps them create a visibility strategy, write client-attractive web and marketing copy, and publish their books.

She lives with her family outside Baltimore, Maryland, where they can be found hiking, kayaking, reading, and writing (that is, when they're not off discovering the world).

Debby's personal goal is to walk the entire Camino de Santiago by her 60th birthday.

In 2017, she hiked nearly 80 Camino miles and has scheduled three weeks in 2018 to continue her trek.

Website: https://www.deborahkevin.com
Instagram: https://www.instagram.com/debbykevinwriter
Facebook: https://www.facebook.com/deborahkevinwriter
Twitter: https://www.twitter.com/deborahkevin20
LinkedIn: https://www.linkedin.com/in/deborah-kevin/
jkgkjgh

Day Two On The Camino
And The Whispers Of The Way

Richard *Brinton*

The heat was almost unbearable.

We had found a small tree vacated a moment before by two other pilgrims, the gnarled branches and sparse leaves barely offering enough shade for more. Like us, they were seeking relief from the scorching midday sun.

The landscape my brother and I had passed through that morning on the Camino trail was parched, the vegetation mostly brown and the earth baked hard as rock, deep fissures in the surface revealing perhaps a few drops of moisture in dark hidden depths. A small bridge we passed over just before reaching the tree revealed signs of a stream having once flowed that way, now not a drop to be seen.

It was early September, and we had set out in late August from St. Jean Pied de Port in the French Pyrenees on the *Camino Francés,* one of the most popular and ancient routes to Santiago, the ultimate destination of most pilgrims through the many centuries. After refreshing temperatures and (some claimed) even a touch of frost one night at a stop in the Pyrenees, we had now come to flatter regions. Evidence of a long hot dry summer was all around and continued in our footsteps with no let up in sight. A hilltop across from us was a charred black colour from a brush fire.

As we sat there under the small tree, sun hats off but sweat still trickling down in the meagre shade and still air, we could be forgiven for a momentary thought, a niggling question:

What have we gotten ourselves in to?!

The initial euphoria carries you at least for the first few days, up to the first week. Full of inspiration, you've made this crazy decision, perhaps with some logical reason – which will, of course, turn out not to be the actual reason, if we ever know that – but just as likely on an impulse that you yourself may not fully understand, let alone any of your friends whom you tell.

Something inside you just says…

'Go!'

And that's it – you have to obey.

Don't stop and question it too much. Your friends might, but you've got to listen to these inner whispers. It's a whisper in you, your own personal intuition, and will naturally not be the same for someone else. Learning to listen to these inner promptings is also what the Camino is all about.

I remember an amusing conversation with a fellow pilgrim already on the first day, when stopping for a welcome respite at Auberge Orrison, a pilgrim's hostel half way up the first mountain. On the way there we had met an energetic pilgrim, Suzanne, who had obligingly slowed her pace to walk along with us.

'Bon Camino!' was a standard greeting, often followed by, 'Where have you come from?' Most were not native French or Spanish but from all countries of the world. There had been a recent film produced called *The Way* which had inspired a wave of English and Americans. This woman was from Canada.

'What inspired you to set off on the Camino?' we asked.

Suzanne related how her two kids had now grown up and left home. It was a new phase of her life where she just needed to explore, to give a space for inspiration. Equals … the Camino!

So we arrived and were joined on the front terrace of the hostel by an American woman (we'll call her Sarah, but I can't recall her real name).

The views were absolutely spectacular, the clouds and mist dispersing after morning sprinkles to reveal peak after peak. It encouraged us to extend the break longer, engaged in spirited conversation.

From first appearances, Sarah didn't seem like the type of person you'd expect to find on a 500 mile journey on foot, but you soon learned to be careful on judging from mere appearances. The old saying of appearances are deceiving, a well worn expression flung out often with hardly a thought, took on new meaning on the Camino, the more so as the days progressed.

Back home Sarah's friends had obviously been deceived by her appearances.

'You're doing what?!' they exclaimed in startled chorus. Sarah chuckled as she related their conversations.

'You're staying where?!!!' was an even more startled reaction when she told them she would be staying in hostels.

'Pilgrims' hostels,' she explained yet again. 'They're different.' A veil was obviously beginning to fall from Sarah's friends' eyes. Sarah, whom they thought they knew, probably used to staying in four or five star hotels, had just gone bonkers!

'But…' Then came all the counter arguments and warnings.

'It's much too dangerous to go on your own...'

'Where is it anyway? Didn't you say Basque country?!' Shudders went down their spines, as they probably imagined scenes from the Wild West films.

But Sarah held out – there was obviously something calling her. One of those whispers, and it just felt right. She also was at the point where her son had grown up and was off to university. For her, it was time for a shift and she needed a space for thinking. Equals... the Camino!

As Sarah intimated, the Pilgrims' hostels were different. There's a different atmosphere, largely influenced by the fact that only those who are walking the Camino with the pilgrims' passport in hand can stay at them. You feel another sheath around you, as of an extended family – perhaps it's the spirit of *The Way* (the meaning of the word Camino in Spanish). It no doubt adds to the extra sense of security that even single hikers feel along the journey.

Part of the inspiration of the Camino is the people you meet, part of it is the extremely varied landscapes you go through, part of it the history and no doubt the thoughts and etheric trails from the millions who have gone before you over the 1,200 years. But another significant part comes step by step, perhaps only beginning on day two, as I call it: the experiences you have, the questions that come, the thoughts you explore. In short, a stepwise discovery of your self. While you of course find this throughout life, it is heightened when on such a pilgrimage.

Day Two is when you start opening a door, perhaps tentatively at first, and it goes without saying that what you experience may not be what you expected at the start. It may not even be pleasant. It may raise some questions you had rather not asked, such as, *Who am I really? What am I doing with myself?* For some whom we met it was a time of career change. A couple we met at the start – for him, he was changing work; for her, her two children had grown up and, though a lawyer, she needed new inspiration.

At one hostel in the first week we met a young woman,

an athlete, who felt on top of the world as she set out: the physical part of this trek should be a cinch. After all, she was more prepared she thought than most. Amidst sobs she related how after less than a week her knee was shot, and a doctor was sending her home. *'Why? Why me?'* were questions which quite naturally arose with her.

Day Two came in many forms. How much it took one by surprise depended perhaps on how much one listened, through the crack in the door.

For everyone it was individual. Some were restless, others were more at peace with themselves. Some were very ambitious, others were more relaxed. Some kept coming back time and again. We met a number who were on the Camino for the third, fourth, fifth time. One for the eighth time. He was 80 years old, from Scandinavia, and quite a character, with more energy than we had! Maybe on return it was the same door needing to be opened a little more, or perhaps he was exploring different doors, an experience of day three and four.

As I sat there under the wizened, scraggly tree, something dawned on me. Maybe it was just my destiny to be hearing this particular thing: in many of the stories we had heard so far, I was struck by how many were not only at a point of career change, but that quite a number were at a point in family life where their children had now grown up. New doors were now being sought, perhaps needing a prod, a new inspiration. Hence … the Camino. My realisation: *wasn't I in the same boat?*

A point both of work change as well as family now past childhood stage.

Another inspiration which only just started at this point and followed me over the weeks and also over the years that followed the Camino – wasn't family in its essence also a true journey, a real journey where you go through an experience and don't come back the same.

In fact, you don't come back to the same point at all: you have grown inwardly, not just in age but from the intensity of the inner experiences you go through in raising a family.

You have become a different person through it.

We have learned from each other, and, if we listen, our children can help us rediscover the child in ourselves, in new form.

With my lifetime interest and work being in education and parenting, the journey of the child and of the parent were already of deep interest to me, and the Camino prompted me to take this to another stage.

This has taken the form of a book, currently with agents seeking a suitable publisher. Rediscovering childhood and the child in ourselves – a companion for parents on the journey of family. A journey of discovery, with many parallels to the Camino, from day one to day seven, looked at in a greater perspective. The discoveries of day two – who doesn't know, as parent, the feeling of, 'What have we gotten ourselves in to?' when the first child arrives, and that you can't just continue as before.

Day seven isn't the goal, the most important thing to head for at all costs – we met some at the start of the Camino (day one) aiming to break some record, getting to Santiago in three weeks! We saw the same sort of ambition in parents as well with their children.

All the stages, day one to day seven, have their purpose and place and must come together in a harmonious picture. I incorporated the journey parallels in the form of stories – to be experienced, not simply thought about. After all, the journey of family is also a pilgrimage.

As we sat there under the tree, looking down the path, I mused on how somewhere, much further down, was a cathedral to which many made their way as the ultimate point.

Some, though, had started long before us – in Germany, the Netherlands, Switzerland, France, and were already heading home, feeling inside themselves they had found what they had come for. Or simply had to get back home! Several said, they would come back another time to finish.

Was it any less of an experience?

Sweat trickling down, looking out at the mirage from heat waves rising up from off the land, I realised that, actually, we were already in the cathedral!

The cathedral of life, built up from all the experiences along the way, and I was looking now at one of the colourful windows, one telling the story of resolves being tested - requiring fortitude and determination to carry on, where inspiration can be found if brushing the sweat aside and listening further to the *Whispers of the Way*.

We took a last drink of water, picked up our bags and moved on!

About Richard Brinton

Richard Brinton is a freelance writer, educator and consultant. His primary interest is in the field of education, and the challenges that children and families face today.

His experience has been as a teacher, as Principal at a college for adult education, and as a parent of four with active involvement in home and school life. From involvement in campaigns, through writing and activities, he has sought to challenge some of the current trends in education and politics with their spillovers into family life.

The journey is one of rediscovering the significance of childhood, as something we can also learn from. He also assists and advises organisations and groups with overlapping interests.

After his work as principal, Richard took time off for other experiences, including travel and hiking on the Camino de Santiago, which gave significant inspiration for writing and book work. He contributes to natural parenting magazines in the UK as well as for other journals, and he is currently working on two books on rediscovering the magic of childhood, written as a companion for parents, or for anyone interested in fostering creativity and that magical something in children and in oneself.

Twitter: @RichardBrinton
LinkedIn: linkedin.com/in/richard-brinton-8ba0973b

Be In Your Breath:
This Is Not A Race Or A Competition

Susie Gareh Minto

I am hard-wired for spontaneity. This is no ordinary boast. With little more than a momentary *Hunch*, I have chosen to store and even sell all my possessions, leave where I live and work, and step into something entirely new.

I've done it so often now that my friends come to expect it.

Some of them are in awe of my courage, my daring – as they see it. Others hunker down and sigh with relief that their life has long-term continuity. And so it is that we are all made differently.

What matters is knowing what makes us tick – and having faith, trust, instinct to follow our path as it unfolds.

In late 2013, one of those familiar endings and beginnings came into view. It was like a long-awaited train coming to the platform where I'd been standing a while.

By the turn of the year the *Hunch* was alive. I stepped into the new story. For the purpose of this book, that's all you're getting for background! This part of the tale is about my all-time life best experience, walking 800km on the *Camino Francés*.

Straight up, my clear advantage was that I had no deadline, no workplace holiday leave to tie me to how far I walked each day. This was the only thing on my life map. My trust was that the next step would reveal itself by the end.

I had time to smell the flowers, listen to birdsong, sit awhile and rest my hot feet in streams and fountains.

My preparation was a four-month volunteering job at a retreat centre on the Aegean coast which afforded ample opportunity to swim daily and walk on craggy mountain paths. My body's memory carried the skills of a few years of mountain biking and climbing on the Scottish mountains, and since early life I'd had many a pleasant scramble on a local 600m hill. All of these experiences served me well for the rougher and hillier Camino paths – and earned me a nickname from some fellow walkers of *gazelle Minto*! By contrast, people more used to level walking struggled on the rockier parts of the route.

All the same, physical body awareness aside, when the moment came to leave the hostel at St Jean Pied-de-Port and walk to the beginning of the beginning of the beginning, I was suddenly daunted by what now lay ahead, not least day one's 25km walk, the first 15km of which rose to 1,450m.

It was eight in the morning and the road was a stream of pilgrims, passing me with purpose. They strode briskly and energetically.

I closed my eyes. I needed to ground myself, to consciously take my first step. What came to me immediately was: *"OK Susie, be in your breath."* As I settled into this inner quiet, another phrase came: *"This is not a race or a competition".* I sighed peacefully. It was all I needed. I dared to open my eyes and to begin walking – slowly, mindfully, breathfully.

All that I experienced on day one, and brought with me in my body DNA of mountaincraft, served me to the last day. And I absolutely vouch for the advantage of walking poles – I became like a four-legged creature, balanced, arms as rhythmic as legs, a whole body activity of upright movement.

When walking in company it's important to be comfortable with the pace. I loved the companionship but I kept in mind the advice of the St Jean hostel host who cautioned about becoming lost in a group Camino and forgetting to serve our inner, solo experience. Being a full on Gemini, meeting inspiring people and enjoying a shared Camino for a day or

more was great; choosing to say goodbye and go my own Camino way was hard in the moment but valuable. It's always about balance.

And it also makes space for the magic of discovering that, on a long distance pilgrim route, there seems to be no last goodbye. Even after weeks of separation, I met old friends!

My Camino nights were nearly all in municipal and private hostels. I opted for a hotel room when I stopped for a rest day, to have the luxury of a lie in. Hostel dorm sizes ranged from 10 to 100 beds, mainly mixed. Snoring was a given.

Frustratingly, there were people who broke the 10pm-6am quiet and lights out rule by getting up around 4am, their head lamps sending unwelcome beams across the room, bags rustling as they packed and left early. They were not popular amongst the majority needing undisturbed sleep.

However, this was hostel life.

There is abundant availability of refreshment and accommodation on the *Camino Francés*. With the benefit of John Brierley's lightweight, maps-only guide book, I loosely chose my walking distances and bought food in the moment, when it felt like time to stop. Only a few times did the distance between eateries stretch to more than 10km. On those days I filled up my water bottle at every fountain and carried a supply of light snacks.

Of all the Camino routes in Spain, it is by far the busiest. I liked being in the flow with other pilgrims. It also felt secure and safe.

I began walking at the autumn equinox, 20 September, and finished on 31 October. My daily rhythm was 8am-4pm with regular short breaks. I easily found a bed at my day's end choice of village or town. It's a different story in the peak months of July and August.

Apart from the use of Brierley's bible as I came to call it, I loved the idea that each step I took was into unknown territory: every second offered layers of sensory experience, at the outer physical level as well as in the inner realms.

One morning, whilst standing with a fellow pilgrim who was framing in her camera lens a misty dawn rising above fields, I mentally echoed her image and realised I had created a haiku – a style of Japanese poetry in the form of 5-7-5 syllables. For the rest of my Camino I created these tiny word images and found them a perfect way to hold a moment's awareness then release it and move on. From here on I'll weave them into my story:

> In stillness I stand
> Sun's new day brings light and hope,
> Earth holds me secure

> Milky Way above,
> Earth's grasp firm beneath my feet:
> I have all I need

As late September's warmth began to ebb, and farmers ploughed their land, sights of autumn filled my days:

> Swallows now swarming
> Warm brown earth tilled and planted
> Wind whistles autumn

Notching up an average of 20-25km per day, my routine quickly became ordered and I noticed that it was like having a job:

> My work is my walk
> On waking I walk for work
> My walk is my work
>
> Body in rhythm
> Step by step I find my stride
> Camino 'my Way'

Eating little and often was the preferred way for most pilgrims:

> An oeuf is enough
> For pelegrino picnics -
> Sometimes vino too!

On the days of sweet reconnections with pilgrim buddies:

> Walking harmony
> Side by side in stride with friends
> Happy as can be

Then in the unexpected moments when going on alone was a stronger calling:

> Farewell dear friend, our
> Time has come to go our own
> Camino Way now

Steepled Burgos draws
The hungry tourist crowds but
My heart is not won

Camino calls me –
Pass through the city, return
To the open plain

Sometimes my lack of knowing what lay ahead for me at the end of the Camino made its voice heard:

Beneath the cross I
Stand, strong arms around my heart
In trust I walk on

Past lies behind me
Old ways of life completed
Future life awaits

Trust is all I own
Love for all felt in my heart
Life's treasures I seek

The chill of autumn became more evident – morning starts were in the dark, warmer clothing layers were needed:

October arrives
Bringing days shorter, colder
Farewell warm weather

Morning sun appears
Warmth sends evening's chill away
A new day unfolds

Lengthening shadows
Herald autumn's shortening
Days, crisper mornings

I even created haiku when I tried not to:

> No haiku today
> Eyes fixed on a horizon
> Far from my rhyming

Wherever my eyes travelled there was so much to take in. The words flowed on, as my body continued on its way:

> Townscape, fieldscape, they
> Slip past like clouds, whilst feet touch
> Lightly on the earth

> Sun dappled path brings
> Soft warmth to my breath-tight lungs
> I strive for the peak

> Old oaks surround me
> Branches form a canopy
> Shelter from hot sun

> Purple heather blooms
> Carry my heart to Scotland
> Their roots are my roots

In the synchronicity of repeatedly meeting my photographer friend, I word-played:

> Haiku-ing 'Our Way'
> Images and words birthing
> Our shared Camino

> Haiku-ing for fun
> Rhythmic, mindful exercise
> Stirs the grey matter

It was a moment to catch my breath when I turned the page in Brierley's guide – and it was the final stage to Santiago. It had always been so far on in the book, and suddenly I was on that page!

From the hilltop vantage point at Monte del Gozo, the city spanned the horizon. The end was in sight. I journeyed the final kms with several people I'd met often along the way. We walked with a combination of solemnity and excitement. In the cathedral plaza, the only words that came were: "Yes, I did it!" There was nothing more to say, simply share congratulatory hugs, enjoy the freedom of stopping, and celebrate my awesome achievement:

> The dream of my heart
> To walk to Santiago
> Today it is real

> Wild waves of welcomes
> Too much for Camino Gal
> Stop! She needs to hide!

> Homecoming frenzy
> Friends rush in to meet and greet
> Is it bedtime yet?

After three days and nights of greeting fellow pilgrims, then bidding farewell as they headed for the airport and on home to family, friends, work, I still had no plans, no inspiration. It was a concern as my funds were zero. And a tad scary. Such is the life lived in trust. Scary and exciting are part of the deal.

The weather turned stormy so I decided against continuing to world's end by foot. I travelled by bus, then walked from Fisterra town to the lighthouse:

> At world's end I sit
> Wondering what dreams to dream:
> Empty now, I wait

> End of Camino
> No guiding yellow arrows:
> Find a new way now

I occupied myself as a tourist in Spain all the way through November, open and waiting. In a momentary awareness of a new *Hunch*, I flew to the UK, journeyed north to Aberdeenshire to visit family, then followed the *Hunch* to the Findhorn Foundation and Community near Inverness. I'd been there exactly a year before when the plan to sell my possessions hatched. This time, I went on a four day visit, earnestly seeking clarity and direction.

The *Hunch* paid off. I'm at Findhorn still! And that, dear reader, is a whole other story!

> Synchro-destiny
> Living with an open heart
> Miracles abound

> If the world is my
> Oyster, then I am the pearl
> Inside, growing fat

All Haiku © Susie Gareh Minto 2014

About Susie Minto

Susie Minto was once asked, in jest, if she was inoculated with a gramophone needle at birth. Maybe so! Gifted in the art of communication, words spoken and written have been her life's work.

Her diverse career began in Scotland in print journalism and later public relations, then leapt into the realms of pastoral training and student supervision in England.

True to the *Hunches* referred to in her Camino story, she happened upon the art of oral storytelling and her heart was won again. She returned to her roots in Scotland to begin this work, until a destinal meeting took her to Ireland. There, she blossomed as a storyteller and workshop teacher.

Another twist in that tale drew her towards creative writing facilitation. Add in some oral history commissions and next she authored two books, *Leitrim Folk Tales* for *The History Press* and *The Forgotten People of Ulster: Stories of Orangeism South of the Border for Cadolemo/Towards Understanding & Healing*, both in 2013.

But *Hunches* kept on coming and so it was that, in 2014, she completed her work in Ireland, headed into a new story and it is unravelling still.

Susie Gareh Minto is on LinkedIn.

Musings Of A Pilgrim Junky Along The Way To Santiago De Compostela

Julie Rogers

On the 19th August 2014 I began my Camino to Santiago de Compostela. However, for me the discovery of the joys of pilgrimage began much earlier. Over the previous five years I had developed an attraction and experience of other Christian pilgrimages as a means of growing closer to God through walking, praying and appreciating the most important and simple things in life.

My first experience of pilgrimage occurred with the *Light to the Nations* pilgrimage walk, covering 163 kilometres from Canberra to Harden over nine days with the purpose of interceding for the revival of youth in the church. During this walk my physical limits and mental stamina were tested while treasuring the value of fresh food and water to replenish my body, any flat surface to rest, the solidarity of individuals and our Great God who creates all things and holds all things together. From this first experience of pilgrimage I began to view life as a journey with and to God.

My second experience of pilgrimage came in 2009 when I travelled to Italy and visited the homes of some of my favourite saints. While visiting the towns they lived and worked in centuries ago I realised, like them I have a unique place in the history of the world. They were merited with the ability to respond to God's will in their lives and accomplished feats beyond their imaginations, and continued to influence the lives of generations to come. In a similar way I began to hope and trust in God's plan for my life and desired to become faithful to his promptings, regardless of how insignificant they may seem.

In 2012, I travelled to Jerusalem to walk in the footsteps of Jesus.

This journey helped me to appreciate that Jesus did come to visit us in the flesh. He was born in a stable, his name was recorded in a census and he prayed in synagogues, enjoyed the company of friends, suffered from rejection, was branded as a criminal on a cross and was buried in a tomb. He became God among us and understands the joys, trials and sufferings we experience. While visiting Jesus' home country my belief in the historical person of Jesus was confirmed. I was reassured that regardless of where we are Jesus is always present through his Holy Spirit that dwells within us.

By now it is clear that I have become a pilgrim junky and the walk to Santiago was the obvious next adventure to tackle. Personally at this time I was at a crossroads in my life and welcomed the opportunity to reflect on my life situation and allow God to teach me more about this pilgrimage of life to Him. I hoped that the Way would teach me to live life better in honour of God. By following the faithful yellow arrows over 810 kilometres from the Pyrenees to the relics of Saint James in Santiago I hoped to be open to and embrace everything the path presented to me.

Being a young at heart but middle aged 46 year old I wanted to experience all the blessings of pilgrimage with the perks of a luxurious holiday and chose to allow a Camino specialist to organise my trip with third star accommodation and luggage transfers, thus labelling myself as a first class pilgrim.

Travelling alone, knowing that I would have a secure and private place to stay, assured me that I would be able to recuperate after a day of walking without the inconvenience of bed bugs, noise and competing for washing facilities at the communal hostels.

Other preparations included walking for at least an hour every day for a year, learning basic Spanish phrases and breaking in the walking shoes I planned to take with me. I am sure the preparation helped but there is no preparation for the Camino like actually taking the first steps.

Despite my best plans life had other ideas.

The first hiccup came when a month before my starting date my comfortable, well worn-in walking shoes began to tear from the seams, requiring me to purchase new ones. Unfortunately the best fitting pair I could find was slightly too small and contributed to an annoying blister I developed on my little toe that was especially painful when walking downhill.

The little Spanish I learnt allowed me to make polite but limited conversations with the locals and although I took a Spanish phrase book with me I was mostly too tired to refresh my memory with helpful words when the need arose. But perhaps the biggest down fall occurred on my first day of my monumental walk. Being one of the most popular routes with the best facilities I chose to do the French way from St Jean Pied de Port.

Arriving at St Jean Pied de Port from Australia I discovered the atmosphere of the higher altitude and cooler temperature set off a bout of asthma that drew attention from other pilgrims by my loud, barking cough.

Despite most of my training being geared towards being fit enough to walk up the most challenging incline of the French way through the Pyrenees, after talking to locals it became evident that the safest and wisest plan would be to take a taxi to the summit and then walk down the other side to my hotel in Roncesvalles.

In any case I felt excited and nervous with anticipation as I took my first steps from Orison and sheepishly walked behind other pilgrims while admiring the stunning views of the Pyrenees and following the Camino markers.

Before long my vision of the other walkers was impaired by a thick mist and after contentedly walking downhill for approximately four kilometres I became aware that there was not a soul in sight, I hadn't seen a Camino marker for some time and I hadn't seen anyone for the last 30 minutes. Beginning to fear I was desperately lost I decided to have a break and a snack and figure out my next course of action.

Fearing I had taken the wrong path I retraced my steps back up the mountain until I came across two Spanish speaking French cyclists. By this stage I had had enough of walking and as I was not confident of finding my way I opted to catch a taxi from my original drop off point to Roncesvalles. After waving down the cyclists and explaining my predicament to them they in turn waved down an older man in an old car and asked if he could drive me to Orisson. Thankfully he graciously obliged. Alas, my first day of walking ended with a taxi ride down to Roncesvalles by the very same taxi driver who brought me to Orisson and although it wasn't the way I planned to go, it did provide some stunning views of the Pyrenees that I may not have seen due to thick fog that day.

Tucked away in my bed that night after a hearty meal with other pilgrims from all over Europe I was mostly grateful that I was not lost forever and freezing in the Pyrenees and the only thing damaged was my pride. Not to mention the loss of my walking stick I had only purchased the day before that I had absent-mindedly left behind when I stopped for my break in the middle of the Pyrenees.

Every day the Camino presents new challenges, opportunities for growth and unforeseen blessings.

My misadventure in the Pyrenees impressed upon me the need to keep other pilgrims in sight and if necessary to never let them go. I found that although most of the time I enjoyed walking alone there was always someone around to provide assistance when needed whether it be a kind encouraging word, a supportive hand, a refreshing snack, or company and conversation to make the long hard stretches of road fly by.

I am amazed that I managed to walk most of the 790 kilometres to Santiago de Compostela from Roncesvalles apart from opting to take taxis to my next destination on Sundays so I could have a rest day and attend mass.

Those friendly Camino markers were a constant security. As a Christian I know my security comes from Jesus but along the Camino those arrows became a close second. Those bright yellow markers taught me so much about travelling in unknown territory. There is no straying from the path when the way is a mystery. The choices are, to follow faithfully or to become hopelessly lost. If only I looked to Jesus for guidance with the same degree of urgency and trust when navigating my life towards a fulfilling future.

The action of journeying to a common destination with fellow pilgrims is in itself an inexpressible delight. Despite our various motivations for undertaking the Camino, we as pilgrims are intimately united by our shared experiences. There is something about journeying together as foreigners in a strange land from all walks of life. Barriers are easily broken and there is a strong sense of comradeship that I have not experienced in the same way anywhere else. We grow in generosity in caring for others as we share our lives, food and carry out random acts of kindnesses. I came to a deeper appreciation of the gift and sacredness of the other and the beauty of the transition from the meeting a stranger to the making a friend. Our lives are enriched by knowing one another. As someone once said, *Life is a song* and we all have a chance to contribute a verse. In this way the Camino is truly an instrument of world peace.

As expected from my other pilgrimage experiences I developed a deeper appreciation for the basic necessities of life. For me I came to love, appreciate and respect the daily sustenance I received. There is nothing like the sense of well-being that food provides after feeling tired, hungry and depleted of energy. Food consumed alone is good for the body but food eaten in the company of friends sustains the soul. This communal activity encourages rest, fellowship and enthusiasm for completing the journey ahead. I love food!

Finally, as much as I like walking, praying, food and friends there is nothing like undertaking a pilgrimage to appreciate a hospitable place of rest. On the Camino hospitality is never taken for granted.

How I treasured the space to relax and sleep after a long day's walk. It is amazing what a difference rest made to my mental and physical well-being. There were many times when I thought it would be impossible to go on the next day, but each day I was miraculously refreshed after a good night's sleep. Similarly for me the day was not complete if I did not take time to rest with God. Each day I made time to be still and the presence of God refreshed my spirit in a way I cannot explain. Here my worries can fall away, even for a short time, allowing me to experience peace.

The Camino offers so many blessings to those who are open to experiencing them. Life is a journey to God. It, like the Camino, begins with the first step. Most of the time our lives appear normal, repetitive or even uninspiring.

However if instead of looking at the little steps, we reflect on our encounters with others we will catch glimpses of beauty and discover God's love through the kindness shown to us by the actions of strangers. My encouragement to you is to find the path, follow the arrows, be open to Life and live.

About Julie Rogers

Julie Rogers is a 50 year old, single, young at heart Catholic woman from Canberra, Australia. Her passion for connecting and helping people who find themselves isolated or marginalised from society is evident through her employment over recent years as a support worker in a busy drop in centre to the homeless and to people with mental health issues in the community. This passion is driven by her deep faith in God that provides her purpose for being and relating with others. Living in the bush capital of Australia she developed an appreciation for the wonder of creation while trekking through Canberra's plentiful National Parks where she could combine two of her favourite pastimes, walking and praying.

After the event of World Youth Day in Sydney, Australia in 2008 she became fascinated with the concept of pilgrimage and has not stopped walking and praying in Holy Places since. Her pilgrimages have taken her to Europe and the Holy Land.

Julie is a simple, down to earth, honest person who is far from perfect but strives to honour God by looking to Jesus' example and following him.

In 2014, Julie had the privilege of walking the French way from Saint Jean pied de Port to Santiago de Compestela and is delighted to share some of her musings here.

Learning To Walk, Slowly

Callum Chambers

Before I began putting this piece together, I thought it would be wise to trawl through the journal notes I had taken each day. What I found after reading them in order from day one to day 32, was a trail of breadcrumbs showing me how much change had taken place from the misty French Alps, to the sheer cliffs of Cape Finisterra. Whether it was a transformation or simply an evolution it's hard to say, but it is still the most important event that has happened in my life and the learnings I had along the way were beyond measure.

Let me give you some background to my story.

I had just left behind my family, my friends and a great job to move my life to London from Melbourne. The monotony of my average week in Australia became too predictable and needed a shake up. But before I set my sights on the Camino de Santiago, I travelled with a mate around Europe. It was a familiar scene; two young Australian lads beach-clubbing in Hvar, avoiding protests in Istanbul, soaking up sun in Paros and sampling a lot of beer along the way. It was a whirlwind tour that happened at break-neck speed as we navigated airports, taxis, hostels and language barriers for the better part of five weeks.

So, as you can imagine, the contrast was blinding once I had arrived in Saint-Jean-Pied-de-Port in the French Alps to begin my Camino journey.

With an 11kg backpack, quite a bit of fatigue and a tingling anxiety in the pit of my stomach, my Camino journey was about to begin, and I really had no idea what I was in for.

But why was I doing it?

For many pilgrims I met on *The Way,* their why was very defined. If I think about the movie *The Way* with Martin Sheen, the characters had pretty specific goals set. Quit smoking. Lose weight. Clear writer's block and so on.

For me, this wasn't so obvious, but being naturally inquisitive I wanted to learn more about myself. I wanted to see what type of person would be revealed as I journeyed across Spain and what transformation would take place, if any.

I had been blessed with a pretty breezy 25 years of life so far and I could see that there was some learning about myself that needed to take place that wouldn't happen without me doing something drastic or life-altering. This was the first time I had truly thrown caution to the wind to see where circumstance took me.

If I'm really honest, I was pretty anxious to see what I would find.

The Transition

My mum always talks about the importance of *liminal space*. A place between an old comfort zone and any possible new answer. A state of transition. A state of unknown.

American Author and Franciscan Richard Rohr says, "If we don't encounter liminal space in our lives, we start idealizing normalcy."

The Camino is the perfect metaphor for this liminal space where you are in a state of transition with the old and comfortable behind you, and the new and unknown ahead. This is exactly what I needed and wanted.

On my first week on the path I was absolutely spent, but that had little to do with trudging through the Pyrenees in a thick fog on a steep incline. Rather, I was drained due to my hunger to be immediately enlightened.

A note I had jotted down on Day Five reads, "I have overthought everything I could think of". I had put so much pressure on myself to solve all the world's problems and unpack everything about myself that I had created a blurred environment in my head that added far more weight than I needed to carry.

Why am I here? Why am I doing this? Is this a test? Who am I proving this to? Do killer bees actually exist or are they just really angry normal bees? Why is the sky blue? I had literally thought of everything. A frenzy of unanswered questions darted around in my mind and I was in absolute knots.

Then one morning, one no different to any other, it all simply washed away.

It was Day 7 in Logrono. I woke up at 6am as usual, brushed my teeth, packed up my sleeping bag and hit the road for Najera. As the sun rose up behind me as it had every morning, I finally felt at total peace.

My almost instant epiphany was that the enlightenment wasn't in finishing the Camino, it was in the simplicity of taking part each day, on the journey. Being present.

In a flash I had gone from counting down the days until

Santiago de Compostela, to wishing it never ended. The weight had been lifted.

From that point on, I would often find myself lost in these almost meditative zones where I could walk a number of kms and not recall it. Time flew but equally crawled. I was no longer in any sort of rush and found myself walking at half the pace I had been. My whole adult life I had been in a rush, but I had just learnt that I didn't have to be.

Relationships

'If you want to go fast, go alone. If you want to go far, go together.' - African Proverb

Heading into this pilgrimage, I had an expectation that I was going to do this alone. The whole *I don't need nobody but me* was classic young man bravado, but after a few days, it was clearly unrealistic.

The Way is full of like-minded people experiencing the same trials, tribulations and eventual transformation that I was. We could all immediately relate to each other, and human interaction no longer became unavoidable, but vital. While I would sometimes happily walk for an entire day, speaking to nobody and hearing nothing but the sound of my footsteps, I realised I needed human contact and interaction. It became less about myself and more about the people I was sharing this journey with.

It didn't take long before I found myself in a small group of fellow Pilgrims. At first I was concerned that I would feel obliged to do what they did each night, feel as if I had to walk with them each day and lose the alone time that I still needed. But that couldn't have been any further from reality. Everyone respected each other's personal *camino*. It was OK to go off and walk alone for a while. It was a fine to trek to a different town and stay the night by yourself- we would just catch up down the road in a few days time.

For large stretches I would walk with my friend, Dorothee. We would go without saying a single word for hours, but we

both still wanted to be in each others presence as we trudged across the dry Meseta, lost in our own thoughts. There aren't many settings where there is no social necessity to fill the air with noise just for the sake of it.

The silence was more than enough.

And this group of companions I had, along with the many others I met were so incredibly diverse. I kept a tally and realised I had met people from 27 different nations! And what naturally emits from such diversity is a vast collection of stories, experiences, opinions and backgrounds that rounds and humbles you. Dinnertime was never dull and the Albergues were always filled with laughter as people shared food, wine and stories. The relationships became the cornerstone of the Camino, and that in itself was a valuable lesson.

The Greatest Test

The Camino itself is an incredible journey. The lifelong friendships, the personal growth, the breathtaking scenery and of course the surreal sense of accomplishment when you arrive in Santiago de Compostela (in my case, sprinting into Plaza del Obradoiro with ten impassioned Italians) is simply indescribable. But I think the real test for a pilgrim is what happens after the final steps of their Camino are taken. How do we utilise what we have learnt from this incredible journey and apply it to everyday life when the two realities are so contrasting?

If I look at my personal journey, I immediately moved to London to start a new life after I completed my journey at *The End of the World* in Finisterra. After wandering through the expanses of the Spanish Tablelands and straight into a bustling city of 8 million, it was a slap in the face, to say the least.

In London, I quickly jumped back into the world of full-time work with the familiar Monday to Friday grind and the social weekends once again normality. While the monotony is sometimes difficult to shake when your face is squished against a glass door on a morning tube with thousands of other commuters, there have been some valuable lessons I've taken from my journey across Spain that have armed me with a spiritual discipline that I would not have had otherwise.

I've learnt to nurture the creative side of myself rather than falling into the trap of trying to achieve-achieve-achieve all the time (something that is often difficult for those early in life).

I ensure I regularly give myself time to feed my soul and take stock by enjoying weekend trips to the European mainland by myself, which have nourished me. I always return recharged, refreshed and ready to tackle real life again. This isn't something I would have been comfortable doing before *The Way*.

I've learnt to take pleasure in the simple things, cherish the relationships I have and of course ensure that I slow down and find a tempo that isn't dictated by anyone but me.

Sometimes it takes walking an ancient trail for over 500 miles to learn these things that ultimately change your life.

If I look at the final post in my journal, written on the last day of my Camino, as I watched the sun melt into the Atlantic Ocean, it reads: *"Wait for life to come, be present and welcome the future."*

About Callum Chambers

Callum Chambers is the Digital Communications Manager for a hybrid change consultancy, *Sullivan & Stanley,* where he has worked since 2016.

Originally from Melbourne, Callum has called London home for the last two years, balancing working life and exploring new places across Europe.

Callum took advantage of being between full time jobs to take four weeks out to complete the Camino de Santiago.

He has a keen interest in sports, documentaries and mindfulness, as he continues to learn more about not only himself, but the world around us.

LinkedIn: linkedin.com/in/calchambers
Twitter: twitter.com/CalChambers_
Instagram: Instagram.com/CalChambers_

Our Portuguese Way September 2017

Angela Cummings

My partner and I wanted to do something special to celebrate 25 years of adventuring together and I was about to turn 50. The Camino had been on our radar for a while; ideally we wanted to wander the pathways for months, and we might still do that, but for this adventure, we chose a section of the Portuguese Way from Porto to Santiago de Compostela.

For 14 days we would walk up the Atlantic coast of Portugal and through the Galician region of Spain. Our pilgrimage started from our home in New Zealand, we would travel 20,000kms by plane and train, then the last 280kms by foot.

We started on the coast just outside Porto in Agudela, a little fishing village with boats lined up on the white sandy beach, their nets and coloured floats awaiting the next trip.

The Atlantic Ocean was big and wild and guided our way for most of our walk. We put our trust in the signs along the path, faithfully turning left and right as directed by the yellow arrows or the scallop shells. Occasionally we passed the ancient stone crosses that have guided the way for pilgrims since medieval times. Brueghel-esque figures would have walked past these markers, most likely with blisters and concerns about taking the right path. I like to think they enjoyed the local people, wine and food as much as we did.

On every day and at every stop there was plenty to see and experience. A great mix of antiquities and modern life, castles and ruins alongside stylish contemporary art galleries, busy fish markets, mind boggling sculpture, outrageous street art and many more fishing boats.

We glimpsed into the tiled and terracotta back yards of small villages. Peeking over fences to see chooks, washing lines, and horreos (for the storage of food), getting close enough to smell what was cooking for lunch.

Hot sunny days with big blue skies walking through lush hinterlands, home and market gardens full with vegetables, the garden soil nourished by seaweed compost made from the acres of dried kelp washed up by the ocean. Vineyards ready for harvest, grapes dripping from the vines, ripe and warm. We were given handfuls of the red ripe berries, ready to pop as soon as you touched them, their red juice staining our skin all the way down to our elbows, and sweeter than sweet.

Pilgrims appear to fall into one of two categories: those walking for spiritual or religious reasons and those looking for an adventure. We fell into the second category; however a large part of our adventure was undeniably religious. We were both raised in Catholic families and share a respect and love for the antiquity and theatre of the institution.

We called into every church that was open to us, each one a lighthouse of their faith, representing an active Catholic community. All of them unique in their own way, from imposing cathedrals cluttered in Baroque style, heavily embellished in exquisite artwork and gilded adorations, to the homely village chapels adorned with flowers out of parishioner's gardens.

Walking on a Sunday meant priests were at their posts and would beckon us into their places of worship. With the smell of fresh incense in the air, we were taken into dark vestries to have our pilgrim's book stamped. Behind the scenes we were treated to the treasures of the parish, golden chalices, vestments and artwork dating back centuries.

On the roadside, and attached to homes, were little well

cared for shrines. All with recently lit candles, flowers and a saint. These were special places for everyday prayer; people hoping for a baby, wellness of a loved one, or an abundant catch.

There was a prominent saint for each area. We soon picked our favourite - Saint Roch. He is the patron saint of dogs, falsely accused people, bachelors, skin conditions and a catch-all of human failings. He's always depicted with a sore leg, a dog and loaf of bread, all integral to his story and sainthood. We brought a mini Saint Roch home with us to NZ to look over us and our dog with a skin condition.

We thought we would finish the walk a thinner, fitter version of ourselves, but only the latter became true. Our appetites were hearty from walking 20kms a day, and every meal we had was delicious. The food along the trail was fresh, simple and abundant. Salads were straight out of the gardens that we walked through and seafood was fresh from the ocean. The small sardines fried whole became a favourite, and eventually we ate like them like the locals, enjoying their sweet crunchy heads, leaving nothing on the plate except the squeezed lemon rind. Restaurant portions were very generous. In a café one night we naively both ordered entrees and mains. We were struggling to get through the first course when a whole fish and half a pig was delivered to our table. The banquet that sat before us was enough to feed six people. We tried giving it away but the other diners were over -fed, too.

Meal times were quite late, breakfast was seldom before 8am, lunch after 2pm and dinner any time from 8pm. Once accustomed to the local pattern, our routine was to start walking straight after breakfast, get to our destination in time for lunch, have a rest in the afternoon, and in the evening explore the town and seek out a café to eat dinner alongside locals.

We found folk wonderfully friendly, smiley and quick to laugh. Always helpful and, lucky for us, most people spoke enough English. We greeted them with *Bom dia* or *Bom Caminho* and always received a response, a wave, or a chat. We dreamed daily of returning to open a hostel and living in these picturesque communities.

The *Portuguese Way* is one of the lesser travelled routes, and maybe because of this the company along the way was always interesting. One afternoon we were entertained by an Italian opera singer who walked and sang with us. Most mornings we passed a group of Australian ladies, whose guide regularly got them lost. Two cheery English sisters were fun, and we spoke politics with an American couple for a few days. We met one of our favourite characters while bobbing around in a steaming mineral pool in a spa town. She was a smart, hilarious older German woman who laughed with a flip top head. When she found out we were kiwis she asked, *"What the f#@! are you doing here!"* She couldn't comprehend why we would come to Europe when NZ is so beautiful. We persuaded her we came for the history. We yakked for hours and left the pool with wrinkly skin and a new friend.

Our adventure had a destination, and each step took us closer.

During the last two days we became reflective and emotional, and quietly remained in our own heads with our own thoughts. The weather was cooler and the path busier as pilgrims converged towards Santiago. In Māori culture rain signifies tears and on the last day of our walk, it rained. In the same steps that pilgrims have taken for centuries, we walked through the old windy narrow streets, jostling with tourists as we made our way to the Praza do Obradoiro.

I wept the type of tears that come from somewhere deep; they rolled down the front of my coat, mixed with the Spanish rain and fell to the holy cobbles. Together we walked into the great square, at each other's side as we have been for the last 25 years. We stood in front of the Santiago Cathedral in each other's arms for a long time reluctant to leave or finish this adventure.

We stayed for mass the next day. People arrived early, mostly hobbling into the cavernous Cathedral, each here for a special celebration.

Before mass they called out the countries of the pilgrims who have arrived in Santiago in the last 24 hours, as Nueva Zelanda was called, my tears flowed again. We sat amongst the pilgrims and adventurers who had made this journey for their own reasons and in their own way.

Mass was delivered from the altar by a collective of celebrants, and a nun coached the congregation to sing hymns and responses in Spanish, while the young Tiraboleiros wrestled with the ropes to swing the thurible that is the Botafumeiro, 60kgs of silverware swung into the rafters to deliver incense and our prayers into heaven.

We collected our calligraphied compostela with our latinised names. Although important at the time, more important are the memories and the people that we will hold in our hearts, these are the real keep sakes of this beautiful adventure.

We loved every minute of it.

About Angela Cummings

Angela Cummings lives on the shores of the mighty Manukau harbour in Auckland, Aotearoa New Zealand.

By day she is a freelance management consultant. By night she plays with words, dreams up poetry, novels and the next adventure. She shares her world with Raymond her partner of 25 years, her philosopher son, a naughty little terrier and a mercurial cat.

The Heart Of A Pilgrim

Heather Gauthier BscN, RN, MBA, Pilgrim
Author of The Pilgrim's Stone: One Woman's Unpredictable and Authentic Journey

Transformation is ugly.

Sometimes that very ugliness is what transforms our lives in the best possible way. On the fumes of my weary body, mind and soul; my entire life had taken a turn for the worse. I was in the middle of battling breast cancer with chemotherapy, radiation and tamoxifen pills when I became a pilgrim. I had already been stripped of my home, job, hair, body parts and my marriage, when I conceded that I needed a life makeover. I had no idea how to create a simple life and I yearned to discover my authentic self. I had healing to do - karma to bust up - and I desperately needed a fresh start. After a host of signs from the universe, I knelt to my soul and vowed to walk the Compostela de Santiago.

My purpose for doing the Camino was two-fold.

I wanted to thank the universe for letting me live by walking every step in gratitude. I wanted to reconcile my rocky past so that I could create a better future. I had a desire to face myself and look critically at why my life had become the mess it had.

On the first day of my Camino, a flock of Canada Geese flew into the airplane engine and rendered it useless. Had I been clever enough at the time, I may have recognized it as a clue that, along with the plane, I would be shedding the me I once knew. I suppose that if you have had a smooth life you might also have a smooth Camino. I have experienced a lot of twists and turns over the years; therefore, I was not surprised that my Camino would echo some of those moments along *The Way*.

In retrospect, that walk was the one-two punch that I needed to re-boot my soul. I learned more about myself during the walk than anything in my life before it.

I have shaped my Camino lessons into three manageable bites: *Body, Mind* and *Soul*. I take pleasure in sharing with you a few of the things that I learned in hopes that it may assist you in some way.

BODY

Heed Obstacles

When obstacles appear in your path, thank them profusely. They are our signposts to get us to look both ways, to listen and to think things through. An obstacle means *stop*. You are probably going in the wrong direction. If things are consistently difficult in life, take stock and consider that there may be a different way to go about it. A gentler and more pleasant way. Conversely, if things are very easy, keep going! This is literally a green light guiding your path.

Unplug

Do yourself a favour and fully immerse yourself in the Camino experience. This is a 101 class just for you. It is best absorbed by doing a full disconnect from your life. Get off the grid and leave your computer, your cell phone and your earbuds behind. Doing so will allow your intuition and inner voice to quietly emerge and guide you. During silence is when you will be able to hear what your soul is desperately trying to tell you.

Be Prepared

Being prepared encompasses everything from being physically prepared ahead of time to having duct tape on

MY CAMINO WALK #2

hand at all times. Here is my really short list: Always have food and water with you. Make sure your boots are broken in and a size bigger than you would normally buy. Have waterproof gear. Listen to your body and rest when you have to. You are a pilgrim, not a hiker! The mileage per day DOES NOT MATTER. Watch for signs. Bring earplugs. Pack lightly. Don't litter!

Keep A Daily Journal

The Camino will reveal wisdom to you one piece at a time; often not making much sense in the moment. By writing down daily events, you are more likely to solve the riddle later on. 'Later on' might be a few days or a few years down the line, when you can fully digest all of the little pieces and string them together into something meaningful. The Camino is *Life School,* so take some notes.

Develop Grit

Some days you will want to quit and fly immediately to Bali. I wanted to quit nearly every day, and what kept me moving steadily towards Santiago were my reasons for walking. Be honest with yourself about why you want to do a pilgrimage. That honesty might mean the difference between gaining the wisdom needed to get unstuck in your life and a hasty decision to head home.

Be An Angel Of Mercy; Not A Pushover

Help any Pilgrim in true need along the way. Legend has it that if you pass a pilgrim in need, you will forfeit all of the miles beforehand. You would literally have to start at the very beginning of the trail. Best to err on the side of judgment and lend a hand. Alas, be wary of *The User* on the trail. I fell for it, though in the end I was still glad that I gave assistance.

Treat Yourself With Tenderness, Love and Care

A lot of pilgrims want to make it to Santiago on their own two feet in a certain amount of time. The distance travelled does not matter that much from a soul perspective. You are walking and learning, listening and absorbing. This has nothing to do with hiking. Remember to listen to your body, mind and soul and to treat yourself with tenderness, love and care. You may need a rest day (or two), a break from other pilgrims, medical attention, food, sleep, silence, whatever! Hang up your ego and listen to the lessons being shown to you. A rest day might lead to an interesting encounter with someone or an unusual occurrence you may have otherwise missed had you walked on.

MIND

Letting Go

This may be one of the greatest gifts you can give yourself. Carrying mental, physical and emotional baggage is exhausting and unfruitful. Let go of the things that don't serve you anymore. Just set them down like a sack of potatoes and walk on. Honestly, don't even look back. It's important!

Be Forgiving

The act of forgiveness is precious to the one receiving it. Have you ever needed to be forgiven? The most humbling and beautiful gift you can ever receive is forgiveness. Give the gift of forgiveness freely and often. The act of doing so might boomerang back to you one day when you are in desperate need of it.

Don't Judge a Book By Its Cover

Things aren't always what they seem. We can't possibly know the full breadth of a situation by a fleeting glance. So why do we often make judgments?

Nothing good ever comes from being judgmental. Just drop the thought entirely. Move physically away from unkind conversations and consciously interrupt yourself if you notice you are stuck in judgment. Just let go of thinking.

Every time that I found myself judging something or someone on the Camino, I discovered that I couldn't have been further from the truth.

Set Boundaries

When I was younger, I would go to any length to help someone; even if it meant stretching myself mentally, physically, financially, with my time and my resources. Self sacrifice was my way of showing loyalty, commitment and love, as distorted as that sounds.

Naturally, I couldn't keep the act going.

This behaviour was due to deep internal pain within myself, and helping others was a salve for my wounds. I had zero boundaries set up in my life, and people took advantage of that. Naturally, boundary setting became an issue for me on the trail, a valuable life lesson I could not avoid.

In a nutshell, you will need boundaries on the trail and in life. Be firm with what you can and can't do for yourself and others. Doing so is a sign of respect for yourself and an exercise in tenderness, love and care.

Face Your Ego

I generally have a lot to say on this topic, however, for the sake of brevity, here's the snapshot: Crack open. *Who are You?* Who are you without your car, house, job, family, status, money and reputation? Try to level the playing field by asking yourself a few questions; *Who Am I? Where am I going?* and *Why? Who am I when all I have is a rucksack and a bottle of water?*

Be Grateful

Gratitude is the foundation of my life and my main reason for walking. Saying thank-you for the good ... and the bad will shape your life in magical ways. More and more for which to be grateful will come into your life. Trust me.

The Camino Will Provide

Many times on the trail I found myself in a state of lack. I lost my way, ran out of food or water, needed assistance or simply felt lonely. Each time I was in lack, my 'need' was met perfectly. I believe these little miracles occur in our daily lives as well, but we somehow don't notice them or think we are undeserving. We have to trust. Lean into the experience and know that everything you *need* will be provided for you. Needs and wants are different! Sometimes you may get both, but you will always get what you truly need, in life and on the trail.

SOUL

Find The Humour

You cannot laugh hysterically and bawl your eyes out at the same time. I've tried a million times and it's quite impossible. I choose, on a daily basis, to laugh. Sometimes life throws me a few rotten tomatoes but I still try to find a way to lighten my burden with a grin.

Humour is my multivitamin.

I'm not saying it's easy, but why not give it a try?

I consciously plant funny seeds in my life, and so far it seems to be working. I would have thrown in the towel a long time ago if I had lost my sense of humour. Keep on smiling. Fake it until you make it!

Know You Are Not Alone

You may feel utterly alone at times, an excruciating feeling, but try to sit in the moment. You will discover that everything you need is within you. You are stronger that you ever imagined.

Find Tranquility

During the final third of the journey, tranquility and peace permeates your soul. I had shed years of dead weight off my shoulders by that point and simply floated into Santiago. Breathe, take a bath, walk barefoot, meditate, go fishing; anything! Turn down the noise in your life and do whatever it takes to find peace ... peace is the stepping stone to everything that matters.

Experience Bliss

I felt like an Olympian in Santiago.

I felt a sense of accomplishment for the miles journeyed and a bliss that I had never felt before. I felt stronger, lighter and more put-together than ever before in my life. This is one of the spiritual rewards I gained and there is still no dollar value for it even to this day. Once you have felt bliss even for a second, you can always access that memory and feel it again.

Add things to your life that bring you joy to regain the feeling. Always have something joyful to look forward to in your schedule. Think of this emotion as a muscle and exercise it frequently.

Like all good things that come to an end, so did the Camino. The healing and lessons learned still seem to linger in the air like an invitation.

This may have been the end of one trail, but it has brought me to the head of another one. Once a pilgrim, always a pilgrim.

From the heart of one pilgrim to another, I will say this: *May you always find balance within your body, mind and soul.*

About Heather Gauthier

Heather Gauthier is a full-time Intensive Care Nurse with a Bachelors of Science in Nursing and a Masters in Business Administration. She has raised thousands of dollars for Breast Cancer research and supportive care over the years, while continuing to be a breast cancer survivor.

As a singer-songwriter, she has recorded a CD titled *A Miner's Song* investing 100% of the proceeds into an education fund for the son of a local miner who lost his life on the job. She lives in Northern Ontario, where she does most of her writing.

Looking for more Pilgrim Insights? You may want to read her poignant and hysterical memoir titled *The Pilgrims Stone: One Woman's Unpredictable and Authentic Journey*.

She is currently working on her next book titled *A Cabinet of Curiosities*.

authorheathergauthier@gmail.com
www.authorheathergauthier.com

Just WHY Would You Walk The Camino Del Norte?

Simon Jeffries

Even before I start with my why, I thought that a little background knowledge on the whole idea is best explained by what inspired me to take on this challenge. After all, just how difficult could a daily 30-35 Km walk be, over a 6-day period?

The *Camino del Norte* (from San Sebastian to Bilbao) is extremely beautiful and is predominately along much of the Basque coastal and farmland territory of Northern Spain. The stunning landscape is mainly made up of forests, farms and vineyards, with some fairly dramatic steep hills with rugged paths and terrain. A beautiful variety of many different coloured flowers and plants, having blossomed after the rains during a wet April, made the walk even more memorable.

The warmer weather made early May a lovely month to walk in, with day temperatures of around 21 degrees and the nights around 15 degrees, so not too hot or too cold. The glorious shades of different greens in the rolling countryside, with yellows and browns mixed in, made it look like a landscape painting. The contrast of the silver Eucalyptus trees and the many different size of trees all added to the wonderful scenery. Some truly beautiful flowers in full blossom made the stunning landscapes come alive.

At times, I felt that I could easily be walking in the Swiss/ Austrian Alps in early summer.

So, just why would you…?

In October 2017, my wife Ania, had walked the *Camino Primitivo* (into Santiago de Compostela) with a girlfriend and they had a really incredible experience, which helped to give them both greater clarity and vision for their coaching and mentoring businesses. They had both been enlightened and been given a stronger purpose to understand better what to move forward on. I was looking for a fresh perspective in both my personal and business life and was really expecting to be guided by the whole experience, maybe to discover a new purpose or help me to decide to take a different path?

I was, therefore, intrigued and curious, what did this historic walk do for others? Maybe *The Way of Saint James* would have a special place in my heart? I went into the Camino de Santiago with an open mind and without any preconceived ideas of what it may or may not do to truly help me to discover more about myself and others.

I signed up with a very special group of friends who then in turn signed up other friends, and before you knew it, 26 pilgrims (as we called ourselves) signed up to the *Camino del Norte* leg.

The UK charity, *Destiny of a Child*, in collaboration with *Follow the Camino & One Foot Abroad*, helped organise everything from our accommodation, luggage transport, meals and all the many things that go into an extremely well-organised trip.

Destiny of a Child's three fantastic committee members, Annie Martin, Francesca Turner and Carolyn Collier all really made sure that our experience was truly wonderful and so memorable, thank you so so much.

In the months leading up to the walk, we each had to raise a minimum amount of money for *Dogs for Good*. The idea being that thousands of pounds could be raised from many different types of functions and events i.e. the most popular being a full-on experience of an 80's disco evening with great food and wine, another was an auction of sports memorabilia. These events, coupled with our own individual *Just Giving* pages, all helped us collectively raise a massive amount of money (£100,000) for *Children with Autism*, by helping to buy five guide dogs for severely autistic children, therefore, making a life changing difference to five families. Dogs need to be specially trained and taken care of for their whole life.

The preparation beforehand was probably key to why I found the walk relatively painless and more enjoyable than some of the others' experience. I really listened to what others had said, particularly their top tips, which I think you would find really useful.

Top 10 Tips

1. Do some training walks prior to your trip; include climbing some hills as well, over a 5 to 6-hour period.
2. Get a great pair of walking boots, in particular, that suit your feet and you have worn in.
3. Get some decent trekking socks i.e. I found that *heavy duty/thick* socks worked well i.e. no blisters!
4. A decent waterproof backpack that is fit for purpose i.e. holds your equipment in.
5. Two quality water bottle containers i.e. light metal worked well.
6. A pair of walking poles i.e. telescopic. These really helped on some of the challenging wet slippery paths.
7. Either a large poncho to cover backpacks or a waterproof jacket.
8. Medical supplies: plasters/blister plasters, pain killers, anti-inflammatory cream
9. Sunglasses, sun lotion and hat (depending on the season).
10. Pilgrim Passport (more about this later…)

The Camino del Norte Walk

We all met at Biarritz Airport in France, as flights arrived in from different European locations, we gathered together to introduce ourselves and reacquaint with good friends.

Because the committee was so well organised, we had been issued with labels, instructions, booklets and everything else that was needed to make it a successful and most enjoyable Camino walk.

We then all eagerly jumped onto our coach that was taking us to our hotel in San Sebastian, for a full debrief, introduction to our guide and for a bonding supper with our fellow pilgrims!

I am not going to talk through each day as that could become tedious for you, the reader.

I thought it far better to highlight the key moments that made my Camino interesting, exciting and at times challenging.

I must just mention the start; we all set off together in a large group … chatting away as to what our experiences for the day and for what the whole walk might be.

It was fairly obvious that a pace was going to be set by different individuals and mini groups, some wanted to walk at a slower pace, depending on various reasons; age, fitness, stamina, male/female company, carrying injuries and just wanting to get to know someone better in a different environment.

I like to be at the front, so that's where I started to walk with a high level of confidence in what I thought was the right way … it was the wrong path! The guide laughed, saying that was pretty normal, she hailed us back and then gave us a mild ticking off in her Anglo Spanish accent, "You need to make sure that you pay attention and keep a sharp eye out for the painted yellow arrows/yellow shells which clearly mark the Camino walk, not other markings that highlighted other walks!"

The fairly steep climb, +300m out of San Sebastien saw us leave behind some very beautiful beaches and head into the magnificent Basque countryside, with rolling hills of vineyards, farms and small villages. We walked for approx. seven hours and covered around 30km from sea level to +300m back down to sea level.

It was difficult for a group of our size to be accommodated in the same hotel each night. However, at least we managed to all eat together in the majority of the evenings.

In the local restaurants/hotels we had some really fun evenings with a wide variety of food, plenty of wine, G&T's and, would you believe it, singing! One of our pilgrims, Gareth, our very own music man, had brought along his own electronic keyboard that was a huge hit ... we each had even been issued with a 34-song sing-along booklet!

The next few days took us from sea level to +500m with some very steep hills. On one specific climb, it seemed relentless. You get to what appeared the top and around the corner was another hill ... *then the same again* ... another hill, before eventually reaching the peak - it felt like reaching the summit of a mountain.

There were two specific near fatal accidents on our walk - one of our group had tripped and partially fallen down a large water drain (Metal cover was broken) having very nearly slipped completely into it. If it hadn't been for her husband who naturally reacted very quickly by pulling her out, she could have been in serious trouble. Naturally, she was very badly shaken and had some serious bruising and cuts, but in the true spirt of a pilgrim she managed to carry on.

On another occasion, a Japanese lady was walking ahead of just two of us and slipped off a narrow wet muddy path, so close to an incredibly steep ravine (70 foot /21 meters). My friend, Jim, and I helped to pull her out. She too was badly shaken and disoriented for a short time. Luckily Jim is in the medical field and carried out some immediate checks and gave her reassurance that she appeared okay. We walked together with her for the next 40 minutes, checking periodically that she felt alright.

Over the next few days, I walked with various people in our group and listened to some of their stories on the experiences they had had in their lives and their journeys so far. I was very conscious to try and listen twice, as much as expressing an opinion (after all, God gave us two ears and one mouth). I did not pass any judgment and just embraced the experiences that people had been willing to share.

I also walked alone on several occasions, not only to have some personal time, but also to reflect on everything in my own life so far.

I am seeking further change and want to rediscover what life's true meaning is. After all, we are only on Mother Earth for a short time.

I want to feel new experiences, help others that are less fortunate. While I am reasonably fit and able to take on different physical challenges, I have a burning desire to do more. I have certainly become much more spiritual and curious about life. Some big questions … *Am I as focused as I can be? Have I really done what I have wanted to in my life? Have I discovered my true passion? Why had I survived DVT's and multiple Pulmonary Embolisms just a year earlier?*

That was the second miracle in my life, the first having been 55 years ago, I was three months premature, born in the bush of Zimbabwe and weighing in at only 3 lbs./1.35kg. That's astonishing given that I am 6'7"/204 cm tall and weigh in at 265 lbs/120kg. I feel the Camino has helped open up my vision, given me time to reflect on life, to seek new challenges and focus on the exciting opportunities that lie ahead.

Each member of the group was issued with a *Credencial del Peregrino* or *Pilgrims Passport,* which allowed for at least two stamps every day to be entered into your passport by either a Hotel, Restaurant, Tourist office or Tavern that you visited or walked by on the Camino route. This really helps to bring back the memories of the various places on the Camino del Norte.

The two that stand out most, and if you get the chance

you should definitely visit the Monastery de Zenarruza and the Cathedral de Santiago in Bilbao. These two places are magnificent and will allow you to spend some quality time in reflection.

I hope that this short story experience will help you to feel the experience of walking the *Camino del Norte*.

It certainly has helped me to reflect and ask questions about my life's purpose and allowed me to identify what I can do to be a better person for others and myself.

Buen Camino.

About Simon Jeffries

Simon Jeffries is a Portfolio Entrepre-
neur. He has a wealth of experience in the
financial services sector, having worked
in Equity Markets (Investment Banking)
for 30 years. His business interest and
passions are across a diverse mix of
sectors, namely a software Company,
Collective Clarity, which develops Machine
Learning solutions for FinTech (Financial
Technol gy) markets, as an active Director and Investor.

Simon is Chairman of *Epirrion*, a Business Development
Agency, which is active in the Sports, Media and Entertainment
sectors.

He founded *Asset Wealth Creation*, a Lifestyle Financial
Mentoring company that uses cash flow modelling,
to help people make better-informed decisions, he is also a
Professional Property landlord in HMO's, BTL's, Holiday lets and
Overseas rentals. Simon is Chairman of *Influencer*, a Digital
Marketing agency. He is an Angel Investor, and Advisor to
several start-ups, a Business Networking App, a Dental Health
App.

Simon loves to make a difference in business. He is a strong
negotiator who likes to apply his skillset to guide, inform and
help people to achieve a positive win/win outcome.

He has the ability to see the bigger picture, coupled with his
highly commercial and pragmatic approach on current issues
and challenges. He is someone who enjoys a challenge and is
driven by intellectual curiosity.

Simon is on LinkedIn.

The Camino Provides

Marja van Veen

Some walk the Camino as a sporting challenge, others for religious or spiritual reasons. What you get from the Camino is different for everyone. For me it was absolutely life changing.

In this article I want to share some of my experiences as a pilgrim and hope to offer some insights into how you, too, can turn your Camino into one of the most intense and transforming experience.

Inner Guidance

"Whatever Inspires, Also Guides and Protects" - Richard Bach.

The most important lesson in my life is to always listen to my inner voice. If you are also looking to strengthen your inner voice, then a pilgrimage is the perfect tool to do so.

One day I heard someone talking about her journey to Santiago de C. As she spoke, I heard my inner voice say: *You will do that too.* I looked at my overweight body and said to myself: *Well, I don't think so.*

Two years later, I got stuck in my life. Something was gnawing at me. It was most obvious in my business, with failing projects and stagnating cash flow.

During a conversation with a friend I heard my inner voice, again pointing towards the Camino.

This time it resonated in my whole body. I sensed it in every cell. The funny thing is that I had no history of hiking trips or traveling solo. Yet it was such an empowering sense of knowing that I could easily get over all my objections as well as those of others.

I knew nothing about pilgrimages and had no idea where Santiago de C was, only that it was somewhere in Spain. My inner voice also told me that I did not have to walk all the way, but that, in the end, I would walk more than I had initially planned, that I had to go alone, stay away for two months and that I had to leave as soon as possible. "What is as soon as possible?", my friend asked.

As it was the end of September 2014, it turns out *as soon as possible* was in the following spring. "That is too vague", he said, "I want to hear a date."

And before I knew it, I heard myself say: April 23, but I rejected that plan immediately. It was my birthday. I would be turning 50 and throwing a big party.

Money was also a major issue.

By the end of February, I still had not earned a penny for my trip and I summoned up all my courage. I wrote a letter to everyone I had an email address for. I wrote that I was going to turn 50 in April and my heart's desire was to walk to Santiago de C. I asked them to help me with a small amount of money. The reactions were incredible. I received money from people that I had never expected and amounts that were often much higher than I had dared to dream. After a few days I had enough money to pay for the first ten days of my trip and I decided to book my flight. And guess what? The most favourable rate was on April 23!

When you're able to let things happen as they will, you'll find that all sorts of coincidences will help you on your journey.

One example is Peter, who happened to show up every time I was at my wits' end for some reason or other. He was like an angel, helping me to get back onto my feet each time I was down on my knees.

Inner guidance is never compelling.

You're always free to choose to have it your way. One day while on the Camino I had had enough of being surrounded by pilgrims. I wanted to be alone. Although it is virtually impossible to get lost on the Camino, I managed to take a wrong turn and ended up walking along a different road, far away from the village where I planned to spend the night. No pilgrims in sight. Be careful what you wish for!

"The Camino gives you exactly what you ask for, though maybe not in the way you thought you wanted it".

Rhythms of Life

"Nature doesn't hurry, yet everything is accomplished." – Lao Tzu

To hear your inner voice you have to become quiet. You need to open up and listen carefully.

On the Camino you are constantly invited to slow down and become quieter. Not only does your rhythm of walking change, but you will also notice that your physiological rhythms are changing. Your biorhythm and the rhythms of your brain slow down, too. In other words, you start to live more and more

MY CAMINO WALK #2

to the rhythm your body was made for! Intuitively, I knew that in order to be able to receive optimal guidance, I had to anticipate as little as possible as to how the trip should go. With as little mental ballast as possible, be open and unprejudiced.

I found that I only needed some basic information and see which route I was going to walk, but I didn't want to read or see all the stories of other pilgrims and movies about the pilgrimage. I found a schedule to prepare myself physically and found useful tips for my equipment on the Internet.

One of the least useful forms of ballast is your desire for comfort. I spent many nights in hostels, but sleeping in a room with a lot of people was way outside my comfort zone. I learned to take things as they are. There are people who snore loudly or get up very early, packing all their stuff noisily. They often woke me up, but then I found out that even if I stayed in bed much longer than they did I still left earlier. It is all part of the game and I wouldn't want to have missed it. In retrospect, it is the pepper and salt of the Camino experience and the source of many wonderful stories.

I said goodbye to time. Instead of a watch, I tied a bracelet around my wrist with a Camino shell on it and I showed it to everyone who asked me what the time was - it's Camino day or Camino night.

The time, the weather, or where you are on the route is irrelevant. No issue to fuss about. You walk anyway and are always where you are supposed to be. I noticed that most of the time I wasn't actually thinking beyond the next step, and then at some point I was there where I had planned to stop for the day.

Walking also sharpened my senses. I was much more aware of everything I saw, heard, smelled and felt: the cadence of my steps, the sound of my breathing, my backpack rubbing on my clothes, the tapping of my hiking stick on the ground, the light breeze that I felt through the little hairs on my arms, the changing scents in the air, the small details in the landscape that I noticed, not to mention the silence in my head that made me able to experience all of this.

So when I approached a town from the mountains, I felt powerful and strong inside. Enjoying my body, enjoying what it was capable of - always more than I had ever thought possible. Going to the beach in Fisterra. Swimming in my underwear and only having a tiny towel to dry myself with and to sit on. Terrific! Made fun of myself, thinking of all the stuff that I had used to take with me on a day at the beach.

I realized during my Camino that I needed very little and that I found happiness in so many other things.

From Doing to Being

"All that is gold does not glitter, Not all those who wander are lost."
- J.R.R. Tolkien

Becoming still and coming to my senses immediately paid off. This state of being provided some profound insights into mental blocks and psychological patterns that had made me feel stuck.

During the tour, a group of ten people was formed. We didn't always hike together, but I enjoyed the hours we did. Most of the afternoons we met again in the hostels and had dinner together in the evening. Although I had planned to walk alone, I ended up in this group again and again.

As days went by, I gradually discovered that all the roles that I played in daily life were already taken by somebody else in this group. I had no role in this group, *so who am I,* I thought. I felt myself becoming more and more invisible, and one day I experienced that I really was invisible.

During our daily ritual of saying what we were especially thankful for on that day, I didn't feel the strength to open my mouth and give voice to my feeling of thankfulness, and then the moment was over. Nobody realized that I had not spoken. So for a couple of days I walked around feeling lost and irrelevant.

At one point during my hike I fell into a state of meditation.

My head was so quiet that there was only my body that was walking. I do not know how long it lasted, but when it was over, the problem had disappeared. It was gone. Before that I had been grumpy, had become unpleasant for the group. Hiking itself had been a struggle. After that meditation I flew up the mountains, feeling strong and happy again -*solvitur ambulando* - solved by walking. Then I stepped back into the group realising that I didn't have to play any roles anymore. All I had to do was to just BE - from doing to being!

I felt like a fish in the water again and fully enjoyed being part of the group. You play roles in other people's lives, but which roles are not for you to decide because they are their own authors. In retrospect I realized that in the same way others played specific roles in my journey, like Peter did, I had done so for others.

The On-Going Camino

"Life is a long pilgrimage from fear to love." - Paulo Coelho

Back at home it was business as usual. But I had changed and so would my life. Old relationships that did not match any more disappeared, one by one. And new ones came. Slowly I saw my old life disappear and there was no immediate new life to replace it. That would have been very frightening if I had not learned how to be a pilgrim. And three years later I still am a pilgrim. Still on my way, but more at home than ever!

The conditions on the Camino are ideal for discovering yourself, but to maintain this state in your daily life is a completely different story; it has become my main focus in life.

I have learned to trust my inner voice. Now I always tune in to the rhythms of life and I refuse to let myself disappear behind fake roles. I do not always succeed, but it's my drive.

And now, because of it, I'm able to fully enjoy life, regardless of circumstances!

For You

"To come to your senses you have to go out of your mind."
- Alan Watts

Each pilgrim walks his own Camino. For me, being a pilgrim is not something you do, but a state of being. And this state is available to everyone. The following tips may help. Plan in advance as little as possible, therefore

- Be careful with fixed expectations and so-called goals
- Make decisions based on what is right for you - your loved ones at home can take care of themselves
- Be careful with social media, keep your energy and focus on your Camino; every evening I only sent a message home to say where I was, not more
- Arrive at the Camino alone; when you go with friends, relatives or colleagues, you will be trapped in old patterns and dynamics
- Don't be distracted by fear of .... anything!

Buen Camino!

About Marja van Veen

Marja van Veen has a history in organisational development and business consultancy. She also has a life-long passion for spiritual development and human consciousness. It was not until a series of life-changing experiences on her pilgrimage to Santiago de Compostela, that she found her way to combine her two passions. With her new company,  *The Hiking Factory,* she offers executive life coaching to business executives based on the transformational powers of the way of the pilgrim.

She walked in 2015 from St. Palais in France, to Santiago de Compostela, Fisterra, Muxia and back to Santiago de C.

Website: www.thehikingfactory.com
Ceremics: http://thehikingfactory.com/en_US/ceramics/
Facebook: https://www.facebook.com/thehikingfactory/
LinkedIn: https://www.linkedin.com/in/marjavanveen/

Bloody Mindedness Over Matter

Dave Sherlock-Jones

My mantra, when walking up the enumerable hills on the *Camino Norte,* is an endless variation of the word *fuck, fuckety fuckety fuck fuck,* repeated ad nauseum.

I'm not the ideal shape for distance walking in high temperatures, only five feet eight (on a clear day) and over seventeen stone (with a following wind). This makes my choice of the far more challenging *Norte* stupidly capricious - this is a life theme. I have found the Camino punishes *pilgrims* (peregrinos) by going over every bleeding hill without fail when the nice easy route is never taken. Whoever worked it out is a git.

I started the Camino on the wave of my fiftieth birthday, having decided to see it in dining out in San Sebastien, which I decided was my starting point, not Irun, the traditional start. I have subsequently spent a week a year following the Camino. Working in the world of Students' Unions I get more holiday than my wife, so I can use some of this walking.

My first year I walked alone. To be honest, I didn't really enjoy it that much. I did not realise how tough the *Norte* was going to be. I'm an experienced walker throughout Southern England, but it doesn't really prepare you for the challenges of the Norte. My first bit of advice is train as much as you can beforehand, it really helps.

I also had a scary experience overheating, up a really big hill in plus 30c heat, then running out of water, not good.

Second bit of advice, fill up on water at every opportunity and take an apple, I believe my apple saved me from heat stroke. *The Norte* is a much quieter walk than the *Frances,* mainly why I chose it, but it does mean you have to be really self-reliant.

After the first year I persuaded a friend of mine to join me, we are both keen walkers and Nik is 20 years my junior and part mountain goat from the way he leaves me swearing my way up mountains. We have worked out that he's better heading straight up for a vape and waiting for me at the top, I go at my own pace, which is how I'd advise anyone attempting the Camino to do (tip three). I find it far more enjoyable having someone else suffer along the route, I enjoy the shared experience and, being quite shy, I find it useful to have the *young-un* around to ask questions in bad Spanish.

The Norte, by its very nature, is a lot more ascending and descending over cliffs and river valleys, which as a balance provides some great views but exhausting walking.

To my delight, I've discovered so many towns and villages that I've loved along the way. You really see Spain, *not tourist Spain.*

My highlights are probably Castro-Urdiales, Santona (a town obsessed with Anchovies), Villaviciosa and Luarca. The cities on the route are also wonderful, San Sebastien, Bilbao, Santander, Gijon being the main ones before Santiago. Castro-Urdiales is a beautiful belle époque seaside resort, Santona is anchovy heaven, it even has an anchovy fiesta. Villaviciosa is a great town with a cider fiesta in September with traditional Asturian bagpipe bands, a float parade of all the different cider producers, and Luarca is a pretty fishing port with a giant squid museum, nuff said.

The cities along the route reflect the regions they are situated in; San Sebastien and Bilbao are very strongly Basque, the language is widely spoken, though most people will understand Spanish. They have an abundance of Pintxos (not tapas) and it is truly wonderful, especially in San Sebastien.

It would be a mistake to expect people along the way to speak English. Thankfully northern Spain is not overrun by

British/Northern Europeans looking for cheap holidays or somewhere warm to retire. Northern or Green Spain is often quite rainy and the climate is more like Southern England than the traditional idea of Spain.

Santander, as a large port, often appears blander than the cities either side, and Cantabria as a region comes across a lot more Spanish than the autonomous regions along this coast. However, the obsession with *Gin Tonic* (sic) in Spain has a home here and there are some great bars for it in the old town.

The next region along is Asturias, cider heaven, they have a cider pouring contest on the beach in Gijon each year and their own dialect, Asturian. To *wake up* the non-carbonated cider it is poured from a height by a waiter and it is the custom to not look where they are pouring - the floors get a bit messy and whiffy in the heat…

Finally, Galicia is another proudly autonomous region with its own language and great seafood, plus albarino, a wonderful white wine. The three most fiercely autonomous regions, The Basque Country, Catalunya and Galicia all play 'International' football fixtures against each other, just to annoy the Spanish I imagine.

So why am I walking the Camino?

I've always had a fascination and love for Spain, I'm a keen supporter of the *International Brigades Memorial Trust* who look to keep alive the memory of the *International Brigades* that fought for the Spanish Republic in the civil war.

I love Spanish food, their culture, their approach to life, I feel at home there, even though I have a terrible smattering of Spanish, not much improved after a lot of lessons.

The Camino presented a challenge when I'd signed off being over ambitious in my career. I found that life was more about my family, my friends and experience, not how much money or power I had. Don't get me wrong, I still love the job I have, but I am happy to keep doing that and make that a success, not empire building.

The Camino allows me to see parts of Spain that most

foreigners will never see, we accidentally came across the cider fiesta in Asturias. I didn't know anything about most of the towns and villages we walked through, we were mostly fuelled by the constant race to find the best Menu Del Día at our destination.

Another tip, get up early and finish your walk with a Menu, two or three hearty courses and a bottle of wine to share, perfecto. Then collapse, have a shower and or nap then out to check out wherever you've ended up for tapas. I've found some amazing local places, beaches and sites, also I can sometimes indulge my obsession in finding Spanish Civil War monuments.

I miss the Camino when I'm not on it, I miss obsessing, looking for yellow arrows sprayed on crash barriers, trees, floors and a myriad of other places. I sometimes feel a bit lost without them.

Tip number five, get a couple of good Camino apps, there are plenty out there, the Norte apps are good for giving you elevation profiles and maps.

One really great website is the *Correos.es* website, which is the Spanish post office, but it has an excellent Camino subsite.

Top tip number six is that you can post a suitcase/bag on from any post office on the Camino to your finish point if you plan to stay in Spain after you finish walking and don't want to lug all your clothes with you.

Also, after my *iPhone* died on one walk, I'd recommend taking a spare, cheap smart phone you can slot your SIM card in to, it was a real pain to exist on a cheap Spanish phone and also a pain to get.

Whilst we're talking about it some clothes tips: if you can take underwear that is wearing out, leave it behind each day when you move on. Also vest/shirts if you have them. I've left twenty or so pairs of boxers and several shirts or vests along the way, wrapped in a bag obvs. Using this method, your pack either gets lighter, or you can purchase mementos along the way. Also, take sandals with you. It is a truly great feeling to get your boots and socks off and free your feet for an evening after a long days walking.

Another packing tip is to use zip lock plastic bags to pack, as you can really compress your clothing doing this and protect it from the inevitable rain, we got stuck on a mountain in a lightning storm but all my clothes and *iPad* were still dry, a scary moment though.

Other clothing tips are that good comfortable boots and socks are essential, as are a good lightweight waterproof, a decent rucksack and a fitted bag cover.

Whilst walking the Camino I've made sure that I also combine it with going off piste once I've finished walking for the year. After my first year I spent a few days in Bilbao, that pretty much exhausted my sightseeing there, the main places are the Guggenheim and the Old Town.

In year two I stopped over in Santander for a few days with my wife who flew in to meet me, it rained mostly (whilst it was sunny in the UK, as my wife pointed out several times) but we did have some good experiences, the architecture museum was cool and Bodega La Montana is a must for the Menu and Marmitako, a Basque tuna stew, even if you are in Cantabria.

Year three, I met my wife in Oviedo, they have a September fiesta that lasts all weekend, canons being fired, more bagpipes and loads of bars in the squares. It is also on the *Camino Primitivo,* so you can get a stamp at the cathedral.

This year me and my co partner in crime went to A Coruna at the end of the walk to see the San Juan fiesta on the beach, a mad night of hundreds of bonfires lit by the youth on the beach with a huge firework display. In the UK it wouldn't be allowed for health and safety reasons, one of the reasons I love Spain. I would highly recommend A Coruna for a weekend break, it is a lovely city. I then met my wife in Valencia, via a short stop to watch football in Madrid with one of my best friends then on to Tarragona and Barcelona, both lovely places.

My other Camino passion is getting my *Credentials* stamped at any opportunity. You need an average of two stamps a day to qualify as a Peregrino at the end of your walk and get your certificate in Santiago. Tip eleven (? I've lost count) is to get stamped, nearly every bar and hotel along the Camino has its own stamp, most churches and Alberges (Peregrino Hostels) also do, I even got a stamp at Bilbao airport and the Guggenheim! Your credentials are a great aide de memoir when you finish and I aim to frame mine at home when I do, my co-walker didn't get it at first, but is now just as obsessed.

I understand that many people walk the Camino for many reasons, I'm not religious, I have no real urge to find myself, however I love it, I love the people I've met and my friendship with my mate. It is a real bonus to find someone to walk with who can deal with my grumpiness and get a jog on when we need to go over mountains, on our first year I wasn't sure how we'd get on but it has almost always been a pleasure.

I'm hoping our wives will join us for the last 100km, so they can be peregrinos as well (that's the distance you need to walk to qualify), or at least meet us in Santiago. Also, we are already planning the next one, always avoiding the Frances as it is by reputation far too busy, the Camino Portugués looks likely, but we might also take in the Inglés on a weekend break to Coruna.

Buen Camino Peregrinos

About Dave Sherlock-Jones

Dave is a Students' Union Manager working in London, he's been doing it far too long but is stubborn enough not to change now.

He lives in Highbury, which is a bit of a challenge for a Chelsea fan but hey ho, he loves his wife, walking, friends, Spain, football, food and wine.

Now 53 years old, he grew up in East London and Essex and frowns upon Essex girl jokes as his gran, mum, two sisters and several nieces all are, however he was actually born in Surrey but doesn't like to speak about it.

dsjcamino@gmail.com

A Fruity, Minimalist Camino
(Camino Frances, June & July 2018)

Alice Copilet

When I first heard of the Camino in the summer of 2013 (thanks to Shirley MacLaine's wonderful book *The Camino: A Journey of the Spirit*), I had a powerfully visceral experience. A deep shiver pulsated its way through my entire body and it felt thrilling. I had a deep knowing that I too was meant to walk the Camino, that answers lay there for me … and my God, was I full of questions!

The Camino exhilarated me with visions of freedom, adventure and connection, and yet the possibility of it felt so far removed.

"No way do I have that kind of freedom in my life", I thought (at the time I was working as a corporate finance lawyer in London and only had 23 days of annual leave a year to play with) followed quickly by "I can't afford it right now".

Yes, I was ashamed to admit the fact that, in spite of the fact that I earned a salary that most people would envy, I spent every single penny I earned. I had a penchant for wild parties, fine dining, drinks, drugs and rock'n'roll … well, "Something has to take my mind off my boring, dead-end job", I reasoned and I continued telling myself that story (very convincingly, I ought to add) for too long.

And then there was the classic "Life is hard, you're expecting too much. Jobs aren't meant to be fun".

I was deeply frustrated, but from that time of turmoil, confusion and hedonism came a beautiful realisation: *I wanted to be free. I wanted adventure!*

I had the Camino to thank for that and hadn't even yet stepped foot on its ancient soil. I realised that I was the one whose life decisions had gotten me to where I was and that I was the only one who could get myself out of the situation I was in. I was the one who needed to change my life.

My foray into spirituality, or the journey towards the self/ the divine (which truly are the same) began with a *Vipassana* course (a 10-day Buddhist silent meditation retreat), where I directly experienced truths about my body and about the nature of mental conditionings (known as *samskaras*): patterns that keep us stuck and disempowered.

I learned about the importance of maintaining equanimity when experiencing anything perceived as *pleasure* or *pain*. I began to become aware of an energy (known as *kundalini*) vibrating through my body which I'd never experienced before, the sheer magnitude and ecstatic blissfulness of which both humbled me to my core - as I realised just how little I knew about the nature of reality - and filled me with a new hope and excitement about the sheer potential of my life and its impact on those around me.

Vipassana is referred to as a deep surgical operation of the mind, from where root patterns of suffering, self-sabotage, victimhood etc are pulled out and I can personally attest to the profound truth of that statement: I came out the other side a completely transformed person.

A year later I attended another 10-day course and within 18 months, I'd taken part in 13 *ayahuasca* ceremonies (shamanic entheogenic plant medicine journeys), completed two 10-day water fasts, a 33-day juice fast and began experimenting with intermittent dry fasting (no liquids, no food).

I began to understand how deeply damaging my self-talk had been, how many fears and limiting beliefs I'd been reinforcing over the years, through constant repetition.

I came to see how *being stuck in my job* was just a *story* and I finally felt empowered enough to leave.

I moved out of London, attracted (for the first time in my life) to Nature, rather than the bright lights of the City and started freelancing online part-time. My soul was seeking long walks and time in the forest.

I dedicated a lot of time to personal transformation.

The process of leaving my job felt very snake-like: I'd shed a big skin and I felt so brand-new, so transformed as a result that I started to look at what else was holding me back, what else I could shed. I got into minimalism and got rid of most of my stuff. Dozens of boxes full of dusty memories. Anything that didn't ignite a spark of joy, anything that I didn't actually use on a weekly basis, was out. I instantly felt lighter.

Fast-forward a couple of years and I'm in St-Jean-Pied-de-Port, ready to start my very first Camino, a 900km-ish jaunt from French Basque country to Finisterre (the *End of the World*), the westernmost tip on Spain's Atlantic coast, in minimal-ist barefoot shoes, as a fruitarian (which means that my diet consists of 90-95% fruit) and without drinking any water (I haven't actually drunk any plain water since December 2016). Fasting was an integral part of my day-to-day life on the Camino.

I intermittently dry fasted for around 14 hours each day and then rehydrated my body at a deep cellular level with freshly squeezed orange juice, fruits, melons, berries and natural lemonade. I'd occasionally have a salad in the evening.

When I hit a city I'd check out the local vegan restaurants (there were two in Logroño!) but generally speaking, I subsisted on fruit. Eating local, freshly picked, seasonal, ripe fruit in the glorious Spanish sunshine, always outside, felt like such a blessing and nourished my soul, as well as my body.

Having hurried a steep descent into Roncesvalles on day one, I nursed a slightly dodgy left knee for a few days but chose to walk through it. After a few days the pain became acute and there was a lot of inflammation and visible bruising all the way around my patella.

Fear and doubt began to creep in: *"You're going to really mess up your knee. It's probably ligament damage. You're making it worse by walking on it. You're going to walk with a limp for the rest of your life".*

I wasn't used to my body *malfunctioning*. I felt vulnerable. I used this opportunity to observe limiting beliefs as they came up and reminded myself that pain always comes up to teach us something (be more present, don't rush, listen to your body).

When I committed to observing the pain - equanimiously and being grateful for the opportunity to grow that it provided me, the pain quickly subsided and my knee healed almost overnight, a powerful reminder of the power of the mind-body connection.

I came to understand that pain is inevitable, that it's an integral part of life and that by bringing up various pains, the Camino is gifting all pilgrims an opportunity to release patterns that are causing them to feel stuck, depressed and powerless.

In many ways the Camino felt very shamanic, like a deep purge, where - through sweat, blood, tears and blisters - pilgrims let go of that which no longer serves them and start carving out a new path for themselves, one based on what feels most light, free and exciting, instead of painful and challenging.

Being in stunning Nature all day every day, for weeks on end, did something to my inner being (something the Japanese have also tapped into with their practice of *Shinrin-yoku*, forest bathing) - it both softened me and made me stronger. I experienced tremendous inner peace and connection and was happy for no reason. I felt so present and *at home* in the woods, mountains and fields. I walked through forests where floor-dwelling butterflies flew all around me, dozens of them, disturbed by the vibration of my approaching feet, through fields of poppies, ancient villages, vibrant medieval cities, mountain vistas, vineyards, over babbling brooks, streams and over great rivers via impressive bridges.

When crossing the Pyrenees on day one I met families of horses - they walked right up to me - and witnessed a convocation of hundreds of eagles: at first they started flying overhead, one, two, a few more... Within ten minutes, I'd easily seen over a hundred fly overhead and many more followed. They were flying together in huge formations and swooping down from the sky, feeding, powerful yet graceful.

It was sublime. I bawled my eyes out.

I loved being a nomad, or a *turtle* (as I liked to refer to myself), carrying my home on my back, steadily making my way to Santiago. I relished sleeping in a different place every night, not knowing what will happen and who I'll meet the following day. It felt so liberating.

So many of us fear change (I certainly went through a fair share of that) yet change truly is the only constant.

The Universe is in a perpetual state of flux. Everything is completely random yet divinely ordained: the ultimate paradox. Every day I walked with my heart open, ready for whatever and whoever the Universe had lined up for me and I experienced so many synchronicities, so much magic.

The Camino showed me that I am a powerful manifestor and that everything I attract through the power of my consciousness is in support of my highest good, a gift. In the words of Paulo Coelho (*The Alchemist*)

"And, when you want something, all the universe conspires in helping you to achieve it".

I wanted to be happy and free.

When we do the inner work, everything starts to fall into place: the Camino for me was an extremely blissful experience. When tension around *shoulds* and other self-sabotaging patterns that limit and restrict our lives, are released, we come to realise that we were the only ones standing in our own way all along.

By getting out of our heads and into our hearts, into flow and presence, we start manifesting authentically, consciously, by design. The business opportunities come and they feel effortless, fun and empowering - they don't feel like a chore. Relationships start aligning - we attract people who truly are there for our highest purpose, people who want to help us and be helped by us. We start experiencing more and more bliss and completion in our lives.

The Camino truly is a metaphor for life.

A few people asked me "So, what do you do in real life?" which always sat oddly with me, since in many ways the Camino felt more like real life than my life back home. I came to deeply cognise that the two are in fact one and the same and that magic abounds not just on the Camino but everywhere. That having been said, there's something unique and special about trails and I'm definitely going to hike some more (yup, I've got the hiking bug). I'm going to walk the *Camino Portuguese* next spring/summer (starting from home in the Algarve) and I've got my sights set on the *Pacific Crest Trail* in the medium term. I'm also planning to walk the length of Switzerland next month with a beautiful soul sister I met on the Camino (it only takes 14 days, apparently).

The Camino opened me up to possibility, to opportunity and therefore to life and I came to realise that all I had to do was surrender, relinquish control, let go of all preconceived ideas and let the Universe take over. I practised being less attached to plans and outcomes on a daily basis.

By walking to Santiago, I learned to let go of Santiago, which ceased to be a goal or a target as I walked just for the sheer joy of it. I'm now practising embodying this deep cognition into my daily life: there's no goal, no destination, only the present moment and how effortless it feels.

I find myself asking: *"What feels most light, most exciting to me in this moment?"*

The words of Zen teacher Adyashanti ring truer than ever: *"When we relinquish trying to get somewhere, we naturally start to arrive fully where we are".*

For me, the Camino was a walk home, to my heart.

About Alice Copilet

An Oxford University trained barrister, Alice left her corporate job in the city in 2015 to pursue her lifelong passion of helping people live healthy, joyful and abundant lives via the art and science of fasting. Her protocol assists her clients to overcome physical and mental blocks by transitioning to a plant based diet  focused largely on fruit and daily intermittent dry fasting.

Also a trained yogi and qualified deep-tissue massage therapist, Alice's approach is truly holistic, seeing the mind-body as one unified system and her system focuses not only on the physical but also on the emotional aspects of fasting, helping her clients uncover the root of their deepest patterns of self-sabotage, to clear trauma and find balance, peace and love in their lives.

Through her *Facebook* group, *Fasting with Alice*, she demystifies the process of fasting and provides free practical advice and support for all those who wish to reconnect to their higher self, access their intuitive and other higher spiritual powers and heal suppressed trauma, as well as achieve vibrant health and a lean, supple, strong body that is free of all pain and disease.

www.FastingWithAlice.com
https://www.facebook.com/FastingwithAlice
https://www.facebook.com/groups/527894747552462/

The Great Escape

Adam Wells

I'm still wide awake at 4am. The sounds of 99 raucous, snoring beasts stretched out around me informs me that I am in the human equivalent of the Serengeti National Park at night. Reveille is a distant two hours.

Or is it? I suddenly recognise I have a choice. I contemplate what to do: continue to suffer this virtuoso performance of the Royal Philharmonic Orchestra of Snoring or escape.

I opt for the latter, even though it doesn't involve digging any Great Escape tunnels to the perimeter fence. I shall just boldly and confidently walk out of the one small dormitory that is Nájera's municipal albergue: 100 bunk beds crammed closely together, with only a few tiny sky-light windows to provide fleetingly fresh air.

I get up and deftly exit. I don't attract any attention and the only hurdle I do encounter is to overcome the prostrate body of a peregrino by the front door.

In the cool air, dimness and silence of the public car park outside, it dawns on me that my escape plan is not the greatest in the world. *'Yellow arrows, yellow arrows', where are you?'*, I whisper under my breath, hoping for at least one to be within the range of the glow of the few amber street lamps undertaking their night's work.

I retrace my steps towards Nájera's main bridge that crosses the Najerilla river, climb a flight of steps and turn left onto the main road – the Camino path.

I walk no more than 50 metres and I arrive at a crossroads. I ponder, left, right or straight-on?

I can see no yellow arrow. It does not matter. Across the street, under the amber glow of a street lamp, a middle-aged man sits on a bench and stares at me.

'Buen Camino', he says. At 4.15am it is the earliest 'Buen Camino' I've ever received. I acknowledge him with a 'Gracias'.

Almost as if reading my mind, he stretches out his arm and

indicates which one of the three *roads* I should take. It is the narrowest and the darkest and not the one I would have chosen. I am grateful: his appearance seems peculiarly fortuitous for me. Job done, is he now going back to bed? I shall never know.

My elation is short-lived: the Riojan countryside, is pitch black and my tiny pen-size torch, perfect for the surgical location and removal of items from my backpack, is now utterly and wholly useless. Beneath me, it's so dark I cannot see my feet, let alone the path or any obstacles on it. I put my walking pole to good use feeling my way ahead. I stop looking down at my feet when I learn to *trust* they know what to do in the blackness.

The night's sky seductively asks me to look upwards. It is resplendent and does not disappoint – the awe-inspiring brilliance of the universe, with its infinite number of sparkling stars, rains down upon me.

I deliberate over my reasons for the great escape: the safety of the *snoring* albergue versus the uncertainty of the unknown. I realise the beauty of this moment far outweighs the insecurity and solitude of the invisible path and this is reward enough.

I continue to walk forward into obscurity. The path winds and snakes over the brow of a hill. Thirty minutes pass and farm buildings appear to my left. Here, there is another crossroad puzzle of paths to fathom out.

But, no man to help me.

Which way?

I pull out my digital camera in which to discover a yellow arrow using the glow of its backlit screen. It is an ingenious idea but futile. I decide to rely on gut instinct. I choose the *off at an angle* path that provides the closest offering to west.

Fifteen minutes later, I see it in the distance for the first time. It moves: up, down, left, right and low across the nocturnal sky. It wavers a beam of light, fashioning shapes in this vast expanse of emptiness. No buildings, no roads, void but for the path.

In pursuit of a rational explanation, I stop to watch the shaft of light dance. It's to no avail. I soon realise I am its intended victim as I watch it zig and zag its way in my direction. Who or what could this be? I ready myself for its arrival, I grip my walking pole tightly praying it would perform well as its secondary purpose: a defensive weapon.

The beam of light engulfs me fully.

From the beyond a voice booms out, 'Hello Adam'.

I fleetingly wonder if this is an evangelical event: God meeting his first born, Adam, on the Great Road to Santiago de Compostela. But no, it is not God, neither is it St Paul.

It is *the* Paul.

He overtook me yesterday and I had a brief conversation with him as he went by.

From Denmark, this was his second Camino journey; this time it is to celebrate his recent retirement. I can tell that Paul is clearly worried and anxious about something. I ask him what the matter is.

'We are walking the wrong way. The arrows are pointing backwards towards the way we have come. That's why I'm retracing my steps', he responds.

'They can't be the right arrows, Paul. Show me the arrows', I answer.

Once more the beam of light goes off in a new direction with Paul and I behind. Soon enough, Paul stops, stoops over and points down to markings on the ground. I stop, stoop over and peer down.

'Paul, they are white arrows, not yellow', I exclaim.

'I know, but I haven't seen any yellow arrows on this path. This is the wrong track. We've got to go back to the crossroads to check.

'I don't agree'. I explain to Paul that I instinctively feel we are on the Camino path.

I ask him if he would like to continue walking with me.

He hesitates before replying, 'I think you're wrong, but you speak with such great conviction about this being the right way, I'll go with you.'

We walk but we don't talk.

Whilst Paul's torch beam eagerly searches for a painted yellow arrow in the gloom, I pray that my gut instinct is right.

As the kilometres pass the tension in the air mounts between us. Not to help matters, my voice of doubt starts to scream ever louder. I begin to hear its message, 'YOU'RE WRONG, WELLS'.

Soon enough, I feel it is time to admit defeat. Mysteriously, at the very moment I am to utter my confession, Paul shouts, 'Look, over there'.

The beam of light's object of interest is a teeny rock, on the far edge of the path; a tiny yellow arrow reflects from its centre.

I breathe a sigh of relief.

I muse, *'Could this be my Camino lesson for the day – in total darkness, trust your intuition?'*

Paul and I start to talk again.

'I must have looked like a ghost when you first saw me come out from the darkness', I say to him (I'm wearing a white shirt and light-coloured trousers).

'No, Adam, you were no ghost. You were an angel arriving just at the right time. I was very grateful to see you', he replies without hesitation.

Never have I been called an angel before. Well, this is the Camino; it works its magic in mysterious ways.

We enter Azofra, a typical Camino village – one street with an east to west orientation – it's 6am. Paul and I, along with a man setting out his tables and chairs 20 metres ahead of us, are the only life forms.

'Dos cafés con leche y dos pasteles napolitanos por favor?', I ask the man.

We sit down outside the bar to enjoy the first coffee of the day and the pastries.

As we continue to chat, Paul tells me a story. As it turns out, this is our final *conversation*; I don't meet Paul again on the Camino.

'On my first Camino ten years ago from St Jean Pied-de-Port, there was an elderly man in his eighties who would always be the last to arrive into the albergue. I watched him for the first three consecutive nights of the Camino. I was convinced that he was going to die in his sleep during each of those night's because he was so frail. And, on each arrival he was more exhausted.

I finished my Camino and then went for a tour around Galicia. I then returned to Santiago de Compostela around seven weeks after starting from St Jean Pied-de-Port.

On one afternoon, I went for lunch in a restaurant. Whilst I was eating, the door to the restaurant opened and, guess what, in walked the old man.

We stared at each other - you remember the pilgrims from the beginning of your Camino. I got up from my table, walked over to him and we hugged.

I was crying when he told me he had just arrived into Santiago de Compostela that day.

I learnt a life lesson in that moment: age is not a barrier to doing anything if the will is there.'

I learnt a life lesson in that moment too: to trust the invisible powerhouse within you.

Gracias, Paul.

About Adam Wells

From the United Kingdom, Adam walked his first Camino in 2011. He found the journey to be 'life enhancing and life changing' and returned home feeling 'compelled to inspire others to experience the same'.

Since then, he has led life changing walking trips to the Camino and introduced Lydia Smith's award-winning documentary *Walking the Camino: Six Ways To Santiago* to UK audiences.

In 2018, Adam co-presented at the *American Pilgrims on the Camino* national gathering, a speech entitled, *Walking the Camino as a Rite of Passage into Retirement.*

Adam is a retirement life planner who helps busy individuals desperately seeking to find new meaning and purpose before they retire.

Website: www.discoverthecamino.com
Linkedin: https://www.linkedin.com/in/adamwells1/

Chance Encounter

John V Denley

The day before we walked into Santiago at the end of my 500 mile walk along the *Camino Frances*, I was sitting at a lunch stop eating scallops with two American students from South Dakota. They asked me a question that really got me thinking about the previous 38 days of my walk. They were only doing the last 100km (usually from Sarria) on their summer vacation, because that's enough to get a certificate. They were asking me about my walk and one said that they had heard it was a journey of three parts; physical, mental and spiritual.

At that time, I felt as if I was walking on air, I was the happiest I'd been on the whole adventure and perhaps my whole life. I thought back over my journey and eventually agreed.

The first part had been about our bodies getting used to the effort of walking 10-15 miles per day carrying a backpack, struggling with aching muscles and blistered feet.

Then, just over half way it becomes a mental battle, the relentless repetition of the routine and the realisation that you still have a long way to go. Then there is the final section when you realise that you have nearly finished, your body has stopped complaining and you start to relax into the journey.

At the point these two young Americans asked me the question I was certainly feeling very much in touch with my soul, perhaps even spiritual, but to understand why we need to look back to the beginning of my story ...

It was a Summer's day in 2014, I was walking past a pub in Cheltenham, the sun was shining, people were sitting outside enjoying a glass of wine and I spotted my friend Abi at one of the tables. Abi was about to leave, but introduced me to Nick and we got talking about an event I was about to run in October called *Breakthrough 2014*. I had been struggling with depression and crippling social anxiety over the previous ten years and this event was the celebration of my recovery and the start of my journey of inspiring others to learn how they can also live their best lives.

Nick said that he had recently finished walking the Camino de Santiago after taking a break from work to *find himself*. He offered to do a talk about his experience at my event, but the dates didn't work out as he was heading to America to spend some time with his new fiance, who he had been introduced to through someone he met on the Camino. As a single guy, I was sold on this idea!

Then in November 2015, I met Laura at a networking event and she announced that she wanted to walk the Camino de Santiago, this was *surely* the universe telling me to get on with it! We agreed to travel out together but not necessarily walk the whole thing together and we set a start date of 25th April. I was booked on an NLP practitioners course on 4th June, so that gave me 40 days and 40 nights to complete my adventure.

April 25th 2018 - Day 1

On the way to the airport, our bus got stuck in London traffic and we arrived with only five minutes to spare. We rushed through security, where of course they made us take off our walking boots! Laura and I got separated and as I couldn't see her anywhere, I ran through the airport without putting my boots on to make sure we didn't miss the flight!

When we arrived in St Jean, the bottom of my foot was really hurting! I thought I must have a stone in my boot, but it turned out to be a huge blood blister, which I must have got from my run through the airport.

Funny to get a blister before I had even started!

The next morning when we went to collect our *credentials* (pilgrim passport), I asked the locals what I should do if I couldn't make it over the Pyrenees. *All* the locals recommended that I take a different route and *not* go over the mountains, because the only way back down, is to walk back to St Jean!

I then remembered the opening scenes from the movie *The Way*. If you have not seen it, then you should definitely watch it and I won't ruin it for you here!

So, I took the locals' advice and walked around the mountain instead of over and learnt the first lesson of the walk: No matter how well you prepare and plan, something will surprise you and force you to change your plans!

The next day, walking away from Roncesvalles, I met Erin and Sue, two lovely American ladies who I would end up travelling with all the way to Santiago.

I really liked Erin, but the feelings were only one way, so this was not going to be my Camino love story.

However, a beautiful friendship started that day and we are still great friends, even though she lives halfway across the world in San Diego!

Erin and Sue often sent their bags on ahead to the next Albergue (accommodation) as Erin had developed a problem in her neck which was made worse because she's a tall lady and her backpack was too short for her back. I am 6'7" myself and as I found out during my preparations, a good backpack should sit on your hips and not on your shoulders.

May 16th 2016 - Day 22

Erin decided to take a train 60km from Sahagún to León so she could spend some time in a spa hotel to try to help her relax her neck.

I set off from Sahagún at 730am with the intention that I would keep walking until I felt tired, but that only started when I was a couple of miles from León and by this time Erin had sent a photo of herself in a hot tub and that looked very attractive to my aching muscles, so I pushed on, and arrived in León at 10.15pm.

The next day Sue caught up with me earlier than expected and I never did get to spend any time in that hot tub, but while I was in town I got some business cards made, to make it easier to keep in touch with the people I met.

I set off on my own again after lunch and had two very nice days meeting new people and handing out my new business cards, before my left leg started to hurt. I should have listened to my body and taken a break, but I kept going as I was having so much fun talking to new people. As I started the walk downhill into Astorga, I discovered that going downhill was absolute agony. The pain turned out to be shin splints, a cramp in the muscle behind the shin which comes from pushing yourself too hard.

As I was struggling into Astorga, I noticed one of my cards lying on the ground. I found this upsetting initially, but then instead of picking it up, I took a small pebble and put it on top of the card thinking that maybe it was dropped by accident and someone else might pick it up.

The next morning, I was packing up slowly as I knew I had to take a break today. The only other person left in the room was a beautiful American lady who I had spotted walking in the night before, so I limped over to introduce myself. After chatting for a while, I said that it would be nice to stay in touch and reached into my pocket to pull out one of my cards, but then she exclaimed *no way,* reached into her bag and pulled out *my* card and said she had found it on her way into the town!

I asked her what her name was and I nearly couldn't believe it when she said it was Chance.

We said our goodbyes and Chance walked off into the distance. The next day on instagram she wrote:

"I found an unusual business card lying in the dirt underneath a few pebbles from a guy named John Denley. It had a website listed that sounded interesting.

A few hours later, I was chatting up a British fellow in my hostel when he reached into his wallet to pull out something. Almost instantly, I knew that this must be John Denley. And it was. It is such a happy little world out there."

25th May 2016 - Day 31

Six days later, I had once again met up with Erin and Sue but by now they had gathered a group of new people with them. I was a little late getting ready that morning and they were all waiting for me outside in the rain. I told them to go on without me and that I would catch up.

A few miles up the road there was a cafe, so I stopped to have coffee as I was starting to feel like I had lost my friends, the relentless walking had got to me, I was not in a happy place and I was thoroughly fed up with the whole journey.

A few minutes later Erin and the gang walked past and asked if I was OK.

I held back the tears as best I could while they all walked on ahead again.

Some time later, I found myself walking along the side of a major road, I was feeling miserable and tears were streaming down my face, mixing with the pouring rain. Suddenly I had thoughts going through my head about one of these big trucks veering over and hitting me and ending this mental torture. I had absolutely no intention of actually doing anything stupid, but sometimes you just can't stop these thoughts from running through your head, it's a scary feeling.

However, as I reached the bottom of the next hill, the rain had started to ease and I stopped at a little cafe where the owner was very cheery and bubbly and lifted my spirits a little. On the way up to the top, I bumped into two people that I had met earlier on the walk, they were now clearly in a relationship and they walked with me to the top of the hill, where there was a lovely little vegan restaurant.

We stopped for a break, but then they said they wanted to keep walking. I felt like I needed to practice some self love, so I stopped and ordered some lunch.

While I was waiting and enjoying the sunshine, I saw a lady walk out of the restaurant, I thought it might be the waitress but she turned away before I saw her clearly. As I looked across at her, I had this odd feeling that I knew her, then as she turned around, our eyes met, a beaming smile appeared on both our faces and we ran towards each other and hugged for what seemed like forever.

Chance had appeared in my life again to lift my spirits, just when I needed her.

We walked to the next Albergue, laughing and joking all the way, forming a really strong connection, like two best friends who had not seen each other for years, catching up again after so much time.

After dinner, Chance took me aside to tell me that she had a boyfriend back in America and she was on this walk trying to decide if they had a long term future together. She could feel the obvious connection between us and didn't want to accidentally lead me on. This of course meant that this was also not going to be my Camino love story.

Over the course of the next nine days however, Chance and I got closer and closer. This is when I found myself being asked about the three stages of the walk as I said earlier, I realised that I had indeed had hit a physical wall after 22 days which ended with my first *Chance Encounter*.

Then after 31 days I had hit a mental wall, which ended with my second *Chance Encounter*. I was now enjoying the last nine days of the walk, dancing and singing and completely high on life, because this amazing angel had taught me how to laugh again, how to love myself, how to have fun and feel unconditional joy again.

Perhaps under different circumstances a Camino love story may have blossomed for the two of us, but that's not how this story ends...

Chance and I said our goodbyes on 3rd June 2016, and she carried on to walk to Finisterre and Muxia without me. Then she flew back to Colorado, where she and Eric reignited their relationship and on 22nd June 2016, they got married on the top of a mountain in Colorado.

Chance and I are still friends via *Instagram* and it's lovely to see how happy they are two years on.

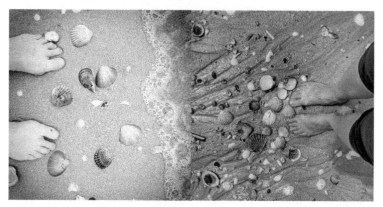

In June of 2018 I went back to Spain to relive the last two days of my Camino and then to complete my unfinished journey by walking to Finisterre (derived from the Latin *finis terrae*, meaning *end of the earth*), burning a piece of clothing and recreating some of the photos that Chance had taken two years earlier without me!

About John V Denley

John V Denley used to be an IT consultant, who travelled the world helping people to implement and understand the computer systems in their businesses.

John struggled with social anxiety and depression for around 10 years, before discovering how to fix overcome these problems.

John is now a Mental Wellness Trainer and inspirational speaker who helps people understand the computer that is sitting inside their heads and how they can learn to reprogram themselves to optimise their life and live happier, more effective and more fulfilled lives by using his 15 Pillars concept.

John is also a qualified NLP Practitioner, *Natural Mindfulness* walk leader and student of Neuropsychology.

FindYourFire.co.uk
FindYourFire.co.uk/Podcast
FindYourFire.co.uk/FacebookGroup

JohnVDenley.com
JohnVDenley.com/Camino (for more photos)

LinkedIn.com/In/JohnVDenley
Twitter.com/JohnVDenley
Facebook.com/JohnVDenleyPage
YouTube.com/JohnVDenley

Instagram.com/JohnVDenley
Instagram.com/ChanceAlberg

Cruz de Ferro

Brad Gerereux

Some people see a pile of rocks with an oversized pole, and undersized iron cross perched atop. Others feel the very fabric of time and space ripple and flex when they come upon *Cruz de Ferro*. The membrane separating heaven and earth is thin here.

At the highest point of elevation on the *French Camino, Cruz de Ferro* is where many pilgrims deposit a stone they have carried to symbolize a burden to be left behind. The pile of stones is enormous and originate from all over the earth.

I was first here in November, 2014. Since then, I have been back three times always with a stone to represent a burden of my own, or one I have volunteered to carry for another.

Today is my fifth visit and I am with one of the Veterans I have brought along as part of my charity - *Veterans on the Camino*.

I was curious to see his reaction as the iron cross came into view.

Our casual conversation slowly ebbed as we came closer and closer until we finally came to a halt at the foot of the hill of stones.

He was spellbound.

I don't know what he was seeing but his gaze was distant. I kept a respectful silence as we removed our packs and rummaged through the pockets to locate the stones we each had carried these many miles.

Silently, we waited our turn to climb the hill to the base of the pole. Respectfully we watched and witnessed as they dropped or tossed or carefully placed their stones. Our turn arrived and I looked at my friend and gestured for him to go ahead. He loved to take pictures, but for once he didn't ask me to record the moment. I glanced down and saw a stone the size of his fist. Huge and heavy to have carried so far. He shrugged and with misty eyes turned to face the cross and slowly climbed atop the stone pile to the base of the wooden pole.

He bent a knee and looked upwards towards the cross that touched the blue sky, then slowly lowered his gaze to the large rock cradled in his hand. He gently placed it amongst the other stones, the other burdens, and stood erect to pick his way down the hill.

His eyes were wet behind his glasses.

Not a word had been spoken since we arrived here, he stood facing me so I reached out to grasp his hand. I pulled him in and said, "Its all good now, brother."

Pulling away after a moment, he looked off in the distance and began to speak.

"I didn't know why I carried that rock home from Iraq but I did. I didn't know that I carried the war in Iraq home with me either…. But I did."

After a moment he continued.

"I wouldn't have made it through after I got home if it wasn't for my wife. I drank too much. I didn't sleep anymore. I couldn't get away from Iraq no matter how hard I tried. All I wanted was to return to Iraq."

I nodded my head in agreement. Mine was Afghanistan, his was Iraq. They were the same, they are all the same like that. A tear rolled down his cheek and he continued talking.

"This Camino has changed me. I feel better than I have in years, not only because I feel physically healthy again. More than that, I have carried this burden here, and now I can let it go. Now I know why I brought that rock home from the war - I also brought the war home. Here and now I am leaving them behind. This Camino has given me the time and the space and the clarity of mind to think about everything that happened to me there. I can finally let it go and understand it for what it was, or not understand it but accept it."

His clear blue eyes behind his glasses were smiling. A vibrant and genuine smile that was infectious and I felt myself smile back at him.

This was the same way I felt the first time I walked the Camino and left my burden at *Cruz de Ferro*.

This was part of the reason I made it my mission to bring other *Veterans on the Camino* - I know in my heart that it will touch others as it had touched me. I know that not everybody will feel the energy of this highest point on *The Way*, but I don't think there is anybody who can walk the *French Way* and not experience something special, even mystical, at some point on the journey.

About Brad Généreux

Brad Genereux is a United States Navy Veteran of over 22 years.

He deployed overseas eleven times throughout his career to some places common, and some remote around the globe.

Some good, some beyond bad – From the Micronesian Islands to Afghanistan he stood the watch.

Having grown up in Ohio, his Midwestern roots and values served him well and allowed him to progress through the enlisted ranks to eventually retire as a Senior Chief Petty Officer from the Navy Seabees.

His career in the military took its toll. Shortly after his final deployment to Afghanistan he elected to retire. The decision was driven more by exasperation and frustration with the politically driven war than it was by aspirations for moving on to civilian life. For that reason, the transition out of uniform was ultimately a disaster.

His wanderings brought him back to the Middle East. Living and working out of Dubai, U.A.E – he found himself at the end of his rope. No hope for a future, no goals, no reason to get up in the morning.

Then the unexpected happened.

He discovered a photography article about the Camino de Santiago and it struck a chord deep within himself. Without much thought as to the *why*, he equipped himself for the adventure that would save himself from himself and embarked on his very own Camino.

He has authored *A Soldier to Santiago* that details his tour in Afghanistan, and the healing that took place while walking across Spain. He now resides in Ohio and takes other military Veterans on the Camino with his charity organization *Veterans on the Camino.*

This account is from the spring 2018 Camino. The group consisted of two Polish Veterans, one US Marine and one French Foreign Legion Veteran.

The goal of *Veterans on the Camino* is to remove obstacles and enable Veterans to make this ancient pilgrimage in order to experience the time, space and mystical qualities of the Camino in dealing with military experiences. If you would like to know more about this program or would like to help make the Camino possible for a Veteran, go to::

https://veteransonthecamino.com/
For current news and information, or to donate, visit us at:
https://www.facebook.com/VeteranswalkCamino/

To purchase a copy of *A Soldier to Santiago* visit:

smile.amazon.com

Leaving Home and Coming Back

Nancy L. Frey, PhD

For 25 years I've been listening to pilgrims' stories. It's a privilege I don't take lightly. Now I am going to share one of my own stories. It's from another era – pre-Internet. It's not that long ago – 1993 – but the world and the Camino have changed irrevocably since the rise of the Digital era. [i]

People often lament, using the voice of nostalgia or by romanticizing the past, the Camino's ever-changing nature. Nonetheless, whether it be a bucket-list trip or an earnest soul search, the Camino continues to be a potential pathway of discovery, empowerment and triumph of the human spirit.

The Camino de Santiago is a tough journey filled with ups, downs, dirt, boredom, wonder, adversity, silence, heat, pain, suffering, joy, confusion, beauty..... It's not an easy pathway (physically or mentally) with a golden epiphany waiting at the end. Such wishful thinking is a recipe for disappointment.

You are the most important part of the equation and your willingness to walk through one of the many doors the Camino opens to you. I hope that my story and insights from my research will help guide you across the threshold through that door of opportunity that awaits on the road to Santiago.

Over the last 10 years I've observed and written about the impacts of the Internet and mobile phone technology on the Camino and the experience of being a pilgrim. [ii] My main argument focuses on how the mental part of the journey is compromised when a person allows their digital habits and desire to connect with the outside world to become dominant, habitual and a normal part of their Camino experience.

Internet Age pilgrims are on the Camino in body but often their minds are somewhere in the Cloud. [iii]

Pilgrimage is a powerful mind body experience and if the mind part is distracted and stimulated by external stimuli, then the pilgrim's ability to focus on the present and being *in the moment* of the Camino is seriously impaired. The illustrations shows how different the pilgrim's mental state potentially is pre-Internet and now. I believe though that it illustrates well the mental burden of the Digital pilgrim in a way that words can't.

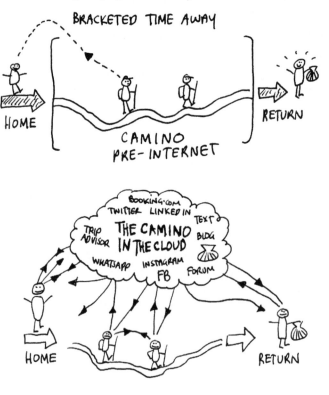

Leaving Home

Digital age pilgrims typically embark on the Camino *physically* but do not make a clear *mental* break with home. It is more common now to have *collaborative* pilgrimages in which friends, family, unknown followers and even the boss come along *virtually* on the Camino. The pilgrim may maintain a significant mental back and forth via the Cloud with this audience.

A boundary that used to be a significant is now only blurred. A fundamental part of the Camino used to be leaving home in the broad sense of getting out of your normal routine and comfort zone mentally. [iv] I'm using *home* not just as family and a physical space where you live but also many other aspects of one's daily life – work, habits, daily routine, problems, known surroundings and even language and customs. As one of the pilgrims I interviewed in 1994 wrote in a post-Camino poem,

For all that they follow the Milky Way,
Pilgrims aren't homeless –
For it's the leaving home
And the coming back
Which gives shape and meaning to the journey [v]

Why would this pilgrim say that the leaving home gives shape and meaning to the journey? The Camino as a pilgrimage has an underlying structure, a three step process:

1. *Separation* (Leaving Home),
2. *Limen* (The Journey/Camino), and
3. *The Return* (Coming Back).

Most often we hear about the journey and the trials and tribulations one experiences on the way. That's the exciting part! Thousands of people have published books and blogs about their experiences. Often we forget that the other two parts of this process are equally important and all three have been radically impacted by the rise of digital technology.

No News is Good News

Pre-Internet a common phrase of consolation during the absence of a loved one was: *No news is good news.*

Pre Internet you said goodbye to home, home said goodbye to you. Perhaps you arranged to send mail to one another and pre-planned stops or agreed to call from time to time. Communication would typically be one-way and initiated by the traveler/pilgrim. Leaving might also be a tremendous relief or fraught with anxiety coupled with the excitement of going on an anticipated journey with new adventures waiting. On both sides there had to be a basic trust and letting go. Cutting the proverbial mental and physical cord was an important first step in the pilgrim's journey.

When I left California in 1993, I left behind my husband and family. I was 24. The summer before in 1992 I had also traveled in Spain for my research on my own and had occasionally felt homesick. I was lonely and I sometimes suffered as I missed my partner. I also met interesting people in towns and on the trains as I traveled from place to place looking for my dissertation topic. It was an intense experience.

Like most pilgrims when I left home in 1993, I felt trepidation about the unknown and excitement about the adventure to come. I joined two scholars and a group of five students for an 8-week pilgrimage where we would walk the Camino and study its history, art and literature in Spanish.

For me the Camino was going to be an academic experience as a PhD graduate student studying cultural anthropology at UC Berkeley. I would watch and observe others on pilgrimage but I wasn't going on pilgrimage myself.

Or so I, naively, thought.

My Camino walk quickly became an unanticipated personal soul search that turned my world upside down.

I woke up metaphorically.

I found myself confronted with all that I had avoided in my personal life and, in that special space of the Camino that is created by having physical and mental distance from home, I forged a path that would ultimately lead me to make major life changes and shape my life's course.

Digital age pilgrims typically maintain a more heightened mental proximity to home and the world in general. One common reason given for carrying tech is to allay fears, report back and keep in touch with loved ones. *Worry from Home* projected onto the pilgrim increases the sense of *needing to be connected* and being *on-call*.

Pilgrims also want to share their experiences, know about home or keep their virtual audience happy with their exploits. In return the pilgrim receives *Likes* validating their experiences reinforcing the desire to connect. That need to constantly reinforce home that all is *okay* or get constant positive feedback about what one is doing is a shift in our attitudes regarding separation in travel.

The old adage *No news is good news* appears less and less relevant suggesting that our contemporary virtual relationships have a greater fragility and they need constant, often public, reinforcement.

Distance Makes the Heart Grow Fonder, or Not

One of the benefits of having a strong mental break from home is that it helps you put your relationships into perspective and what they mean to you. Keeping yourself mentally connected, you don't give yourself a chance to miss loved ones fully or have sufficient mental distance from them to see the relationships clearly.

As I embarked on my Camino in 1993, I knew I would miss my mother very much as she and I were very close and spoke frequently on the phone. If she and I had the same relationship then and phones had existed, we would have *messaged* and *Skyped* each other constantly about all of my insecurities, observations and doubts.

At the time I was also deeply bonded with my husband of one year who had been my steady boyfriend prior to that since we were 14 and 15. We had never broken up in all those years. We were best friends and loved each other very much. If I had had a phone, he and I would also have been constantly chatting via a messaging platform keeping me from the group, my experience of where I was and my Camino. I probably also would have been texting grad school friends, my professors for advice and shared photos on Instagram. My mind would have been all over the place except where I was physically.

Connection via the Internet can provide tremendous support for a pilgrim especially when feeling down, tired, insecure, or lonely. The temptation and the ease with which you can resolve those negative feelings through a phone reduces the need for the pilgrim to look within to find a solution or look around to fellow companions or circumstances.

Pilgrims appear more independent but actually become more isolated from their on-the-ground community and more dependent on their phone and virtual community to resolve crises. The consequence is self-limitation and distance from the present moment. Curiously, what on the surface appears to be a help may actually be a hindrance to growth, as the quick-fix is not always the best solution for long-lasting inner solace. Your phone may end up being the heaviest weight in your pack.

While I loved my husband very much part of me unconsciously knew that I had not been completely honest with him or myself about my doubts I had about our relationship. I knew that there was something untapped within me that, up to that point, our relationship had been unable to access. He was my best friend. We shared everything together. I loved him dearly. I did not want to throw that out the window because of some unknown curiosity which I assumed was some defect within me that had no solution.

What does this have to do with my Camino? Everything and nothing. The Camino often isn't about what we think it will be.

I love the quote from Bunyan's *The Pilgrim's Progress* that starts the book:

"As I walked through the wilderness of this world …". [vi]

The wilderness he walks into is his own inner world that is a fearful, unknown place. How will he react when confronted with temptation, adversity and the unknown? You must face the fear to move forward.

I called one of my chapters in *Pilgrim Stories, Landscapes of Discovery* because that is often what the Camino is - a space of discovery, surprise and wonder when we allow ourselves to delve into our unknown, inner realms.

Getting into the simple rhythm of the Camino of walking, eating, finding shelter and sleeping allows the pilgrim to receive two of the Camino's greatest gifts: the power of simplicity and freed up mental space.

People love the simplicity of the Camino and how you can feel deeply fulfilled and connected with the world and those around you when you have relatively few material possessions even if you are suffering physically.

By *freed up mental space* I don't mean a clear mind without thoughts – though some people may experience that as well - I mean the layer of stress that one carries around in daily life induced by work, responsibilities, commitments, busy-ness, contemporary society, etc is lifted.

A mental pairing down typically occurs after a few days of walking when your mind is anchored to the present and not drawn constantly to the worries of the world. Into that freed up space, inner material often surfaces and flows – upwellings of emotion, memories of the past, vivid dreams, confusing thoughts, people you once knew, songs, etc.

In my book *Pilgrim Stories* I describe this as a cork being released from a bottle. If this freed up space is constantly filled with noise from the Internet or the perceived need to please the home audience with status updates and social media posts, the pilgrim never allows him/herself to release the cork of stress and see what lies underneath. You don't give yourself a chance get out of the rut of your mental routine.

The Mental Distance Allowed Me To Find Myself

On the surface I had a normal Camino walking along, learning, meeting other people, feeling wonder and awe at the historical monuments we passed, enjoying the natural landscapes, suffering pains in my feet, etc.

On the inside I was an emotional wreck.

Within the group of five students there was someone I felt an instant, magnetic attraction to. It was so intense it was painful. I felt a profound inner turmoil. That untapped part of me was screaming out for me to take action but my love, fidelity and respect for my partner shouted equally strongly to stay away from this with a 10-ft pole. It was agonizing and there was no one I wanted to confide in nearby. It was hard but I am glad it was that way. If it were today and I had had a phone, I would have been *texting* and *Skypeing* my husband and my mother and the potential guilt and mental proximity probably would have altered the outcome significantly. I thought my Camino was a disaster due to this unforeseen life situation. But this was my Camino. I had to confront what I had been unable to see clearly in my daily life. I was profoundly dissatisfied on some essential level with what I thought was my perfect relationship. As hard as it was, the distance (emotional and physical) allowed me to access this place within myself, a place I really didn't want to go.

It turned out the attraction with the other person in the group was mutual. He would place his hand on my back and I felt electricity. I had never felt like that. After struggling I decided I had to listen to this inner urge that compelled me so strongly.

One evening we took a walk and wandered to edge of the village. At one point we turned to one another and kissed. I literally saw fireworks like in a movie. The inner charge was equally strong. I had never felt anything like that before. It was intoxicating and confirmed all of my inner doubts that I had denied myself for many years. He became my catalyst for change. As I write this I can easily conjure the emotion of this moment probably because I have never written about it before. I've told a few people orally but there are simply stories one keeps to oneself. The more you tell a story, the more the power and energy around the story potentially changes and diminishes.

While on one hand I felt I had seen the light on the other I was wracked by a terrible sense of guilt. The *OneRepublic's* song from a few years ago *Counting Stars* instantly resonated when I heard it for the first time:

I, feel something so right
Doing the wrong thing
I, feel something so wrong
But doing the right thing [vii]

Achieving this mental state becomes the access point to inner understanding and allows you to observe your own life. People had monkey-mind (i.e., overly active and easily distracted) too back then just like they do now.

Releasing the cork is not necessarily a pleasant experience. In fact it can be fairly traumatic.

The big difference between pre-Internet and now was when it got mentally tough on the Camino you couldn't escape into the Internet. You had to deal one way or another in the present. People did escape mentally into books they might carry or alcohol, or relationships along the *Way* but still their minds were anchored in that place and space and not distracted by *Facebook* posts, Internet dating sites, sports channels, *TripAdvisor* bookings, notifications, *SnapChat* images, frustrations with crappy WiFi, blogs, sharing photos on *Instagram,* etc, etc, etc. All these things serve to keep you on the surface of your life. People talk now about the Camino being stressful because they don't have enough time to write it all down and share it. You don't have to share it, you can simply live it.

The Camino becomes work rather than something you live and breathe, suffer and enjoy.

The Gift of Feeling Alone and Far, Far Away

One of my most powerful memories from my first Camino in 1993 was walking across the *meseta* (Spain's high tableland between Burgos and León) on a moonlight night with several companions. At one point we reached a rise and huge wheat field extended out in front of us. We went into the wheat, laid down on our backs and looked up at the star-filled sky. I remember feeling a powerful sense of freedom and anonymity and the thought went through my head, "No one in the world knows where I am right now." It was very liberating. I was just one with the stars, insignificant in this vast, open space and all was good.

If it were now, I'd want to share it, or take a selfie of myself and my friends or start thinking about how I would write about it in a blog. It was just a moment to live that has always stayed with me in a powerful, comforting way.

Over the years, guiding people along this stretch of the Camino, I have probably passed this place 75 times and I always look on that field and remember that moment with a sense of great inner peace. Sometimes the wheat is lush. Sometimes it's been harvested. Sometimes there are red poppies coming up through the stalks. Windfarms have gone up in the distance on the horizon. It doesn't matter, the essence of the place and the moment are still there embedded in my inner Camino landscape. I wonder if I would even remember this moment if I had tossed it into wind of the Cloud with all my other amazing moments back in 1993?

Pre-Internet you could be a different person and experience new and different things without judgment or ties or worry about what *home* might think. If you are constantly reporting back, you may inhibit yourself from experimenting with self and others. Your journey is no longer your own when you have a host of people watching you from the Cloud and you are editing your experiences as they are happening.

The truth is there is a part of pilgrimage which is very selfish – it's typically a journey you need to go on alone mentally to have a true time-out from your life, responsibilities and worries to achieve the mental pairing down and stillness within that brings connection, insight and transformation. Sometimes you just need time for you, however you may define the journey's purpose whether it be religious, spiritual, inner or personal. We need to withdraw from the cares of the world and simply be – sit in the wheat, look at the sky, listen to your body and the sounds of nature, be still and wonder.

Leaving Home is Hard, Returning Can Be Worse

Over the following weeks I allowed my instincts to flow and to trust my inner world and where it was taking me. At the same time I was wracked with guilt. I knew something very powerful was occurring, I had some idea of where it might lead me and I was terrified. I was worried on one hand about the future and exultant and powerfully energized in the present of the Camino.

My dream life was very vivid. I wrote in my journal. I felt the present greatly. I saw my life clearly and made other decisions too. I wrote letters and received letters at periodic stops along the way about stuff that had no relevance. I took about eight rolls of colour slides that I wouldn't see for another two months.

About five weeks into the trip I felt like I had to talk to my mother to get some perspective. I made an expensive international phone call and heard the calming voice of my mom telling me it would work out.

I also remember reflecting that the previous summer on my own in Spain I had experienced intense homesickness but this summer on the Camino I simply didn't want it to end. As the weeks went on the intensity of emotion was so great that I decided I had to stop it before the relationship with the catalyst got more serious than I wanted. The door had been opened, the spring tapped, my eyes uncovered. There was no going back to my previous state. I had experienced a profound internal shift over the course of the pilgrimage.

As I reflected in the last days about all that had happened over the previous eight weeks, my goal upon return was to incorporate this intense new energy into my relationship with my husband. I did not want to lose him or what we had. I never would have guessed before starting the Camino that my graduate school research project would have as an outcome a profound personal dilemma around one of the things I felt most confident about before leaving – my relationship with my husband.

All of this time I did not have any contact with the outside world except a few glances at the TV in bars, letters from home and one or two phone calls over 8-weeks. My mind was profoundly centered in and on the Camino for eight-weeks. I achieved a powerful experience of the here and the now. I was not multi-tasking my Camino by sharing the many moments of the day. I did not send emails or write a blog to get feedback. I didn't parcel it out in fragments as it was occurring. I kept this inside of me evolving, growing and churning. I didn't worry, like I would today, that I wouldn't remember everything or try to record it all. I didn't feel stressed out about not having time to share my experiences. I wasn't trying to process my experiences by writing emails to others and getting feedback.

Believe me, I didn't do this because I wouldn't have wanted to but because it simply wasn't possible. I feel very lucky to have been stuck in this mental bubble because it takes a tremendous amount of discipline now not to give into the temptation to connect to the Internet and share or get help as we do now. The energy and time that Digital pilgrims now invest in Cloud activities is startling.

My well laid plans for my return failed miserably. Nothing was the same. I wasn't the same. The spring that had been tapped would not stop flowing but when I tried to incorporate it into the relationship the flow dried up. The relationship couldn't contain the shifts and changes. I was faced with devastating choices – close my eyes to what had been revealed and save our relationship but die on the inside in the process or keep my eyes open and take the plunge into the abyss of uncertainty that lay ahead by ending what was a beautiful relationship.

In the months after my return, I developed a very strong inner image: I was standing on an enormous, vast open plain and in the far distance I could see this radiant city, glittering. Between me and this vision of promise was a vast, black canyon. I walked to the edge of the canyon and looked down into the abyss and darkness but could see no way across. The only way to get to the other side was to go down into that pit of fear and uncertainty and climb back up the other side. I didn't want to go and turned around and looked back but there was nothing there – just empty plain. It was the hardest emotional leap I ever took in my life. I flung myself into that black space and I managed to crawl back out onto the other side. I didn't climb out unscathed nor did those in my circle. I ended up breaking my husband's heart in the process and shocking everyone in my circle of friends and family. I had always been the straight, reliable arrow. Some of them have never forgiven me.

All of these years later, I still feel bad for him and always wished that it had been a mutual decision. I never wanted to hurt anyone on my journey but sometimes that is the outcome of profound growth and change for the spirit to survive and thrive.

At the same time, I never regretted descending into the chasm and I feel very grateful to the Camino for the many gifts I received along the way. I grew up on the Camino. The mental and physical time away allowed me to separate and become my own person. It was very hard and I was not the same person when I returned. I was a stronger, more confident and capable version of myself. I felt an iron bar of courage running through my centre that allowed me to make the changes that I did. I was also more compassionate and less judgmental.

I returned to the Camino to do my field research from July 1994 to Aug 1995 working as an hospitalera in many albergues along the way. The outcome of my conversations, listening and tending pilgrims was *Pilgrim Stories*.

Since I had already been through my own personal Camino hell and survived, it allowed me to be a better caregiver as well as a compassionate listener and more understanding of pilgrims' inner struggles. I am still friends with many pilgrims I met in those profound months of research in the 1990s when I was often the only person who heard a pilgrim's story because, unlike today, people didn't share and post their experiences as they went. There's great power in keeping your stories and experiences inside and letting them churn and evolve within you until you are ready to reflect on and learn from them.

The Journey Goes On

What does this have to do with tech?

I can confidently say that I never would have undergone the powerful transformation I experienced on the Camino in 1993 if I had been connected to the Internet.

People really aren't all that different mentally today than they were 25 years ago. Now, like then, there are many insecure, needy, adventure seeking, confused, curious, hopeful people who are open or closed to new experiences on the Camino. The big difference between then and now is that pre-Internet you were forced by circumstances to deal with all of your issues, adversities, inner anxieties, etc in a contained space limited almost entirely to the immediate world around you. It was easier to reach that state and maintain it even if you didn't want to. I'm definitely not saying that everyone chose to keep their eyes open or take their Camino lessons fully home. Many people compartmentalized and some seemed to learn nothing or left the Camino when the going got rough.

Nonetheless, that fact is you couldn't escape from yourself or the Camino as easily as you can now. Circumstances forced you to look within to deal with whatever adversity arose and thereby the Camino gave you constant opportunities to grow, struggle and learn. If you struggled with loneliness you turned to your companions or the hospitaleros or villagers and other people you met along the way. If you got lost you fought down the panic and figured it out. Each of these experiences often became life lessons to help you deal better in the real world.

In the Internet Age, the tendency is to instantly resolve any minor glitch by turning to your phone for the solution. We diminish our Camino tremendously when we don't allow ourselves to have one. If you don't live, you don't learn. Our phones keep us from living by dulling our senses. When we delegate our emotional needs to our phones, we miss opportunities to grow and at the same time atrophy our dealing-with-life skills in the process through disuse.

If you never really leave home, what's the point of going on pilgrimage as a time-out, soul search or personal, transformative journey? Dare to enter the wilderness within.

I don't guarantee you won't come out unscathed but you will definitely learn many things along the way.

References

i. I'm using roughly the year 2000 but on the Camino the Internet's impact didn't really become visible until about 2008.

ii. Please see my website *Walking to Presence (www.walkingtopresence.com)* where I share my research on pilgrimage in the Internet Age.

iii. On my website *Walking to Presence (www.walkingtopresence.com)*, you will find the article *15 Tips for Keeping Your Head Out of the Cloud* if you want to reflect on how digital communications potentially impact your Camino experience.

iv. Fortunately, people still get out of their routines through the physical journey which is often very tough and requires mental fortitude. Both being in nature and walking are powerful therapeutic activities which are also conducive to helping the pilgrim access his/her inner worlds.

v. Frey, N. (1998). *Pilgrim Stories. On and Off the Road to Santiago.* UC Press, p. 178

vi. Bunyan, J. (1853). *The Pilgrim's Progress.* Auburn: Derby & Miller, p. 10.

vii. Songwriter: Tedder, R. (2013). Lyrics from *Counting Stars* by OneRepbulic © Sony/ATV Music Publishing LLC.

About Nancy Frey PhD

In 1998 Nancy published *Pilgrim Stories. On and Off the Road to Santiago* (UC Press, 1998) based on her three-year anthropological research project on the Camino de Santiago pilgrimage in the early 1990s.

She received her PhD in Cultural Anthropology from UC Berkeley in 1996.

In *Pilgrim Stories*, Nancy brings to life the multi-faceted nature of the late 20th C pilgrim experience and takes the reader through the pilgrim's journey before, during and after the Camino is over.

Nancy moved to Spain in 1998 and began to write for *Lonely Planet* as well lecture for the Smithsonian Institution and the University of Santiago de Compostela.

In 1999, she founded the educational walking tours company *On Foot in Spain* (*www.onfootinspain.com*) with her partner. Since then Nancy has shared with more than 1400 people her knowledge, love and passion for the Camino on their guided tours and walked the Camino too many times to count.

Nancy's 25-year relationship with the Camino spans the rise of the Internet. Witnessing and observing the changes wrought by an increasingly digitalized society, Nancy began to research the impacts of the Digital Age on the Camino. She freely shares her research on this topic on her website: *Walking to Presence* (*www.walkingtopresence.com*).

On Foot in Spain (www.onfootinspain.com)
Walking to Presence (www.walkingtopresence.com)

Would You Like To Share Your Camino Story?

My Camino Walk is a #1 ranked and bestselling *Travel and Tourism, Hikes and Walks, Hospitality* and even *Self Help* Amazon series.

We are now calling for authors for the next *My Camino Walk*.

Here's how it works.

Basically, we need around 1,500 words. Your story should be an original story that shares your Camino journey, your insights, your tips and your experience. We also need a bio - 200 words about you - some links, a high res JPEG headshot (600kb+) and maybe one or two photos of your trip.

There is a very small token fee to participate but this covers admin and some of the set-up costs.

If you'd like to know more email *coachbiz@hotmail.com* and we will send you the *My Camino Walk Writers Guide*.

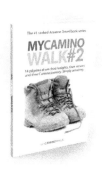

Did You Miss Earlier Editions of My Camino Walk?

The *My Camino Walk* series of books are available on Kindle as an e-book and on Amazon as a paperback worldwide.

Search *www.amazon.com*